Come swim with me to my island …

RAINBOWS OVER KAPA'A

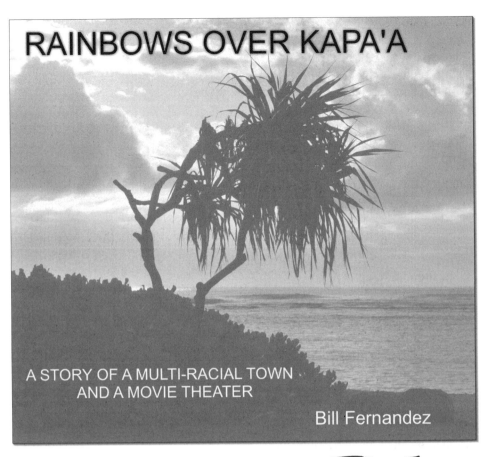

RAINBOWS OVER KAPA'A

A STORY OF A MULTI-RACIAL TOWN
AND A MOVIE THEATER

Bill Fernandez

Me Ko aloha pu me kana. Bill Fernandez

Printed in United States of America
First Printing 2009

Library of Congress Cataloging-in-Publication Data
Pending as of this printing

Fernandez, Bill
   Rainbows Over Kapa'a / Bill Fernandez
   Includes index.
   SAN: 857-2577
   ISBN 978-0-615-30211-9 (pbk. :alk. paper)
   1. Title: Rainbows Over Kapa'a

Designed by Bill, Judie, and Jon Fernandez, Tammi Andersland,
and John Lydgate

Cover Photographs Judith Fernandez

Printed by Hagadone Printing Company
274 Pu'uhale Road
Honolulu, HI 96819

Web Site:www.wfernandez.com

Central Pacific Media Corporation

printed carbon neutral
www.natureOffice.com / US-180-462601

FOREWORD

Not much has been written about the sleepy, bucolic town of Kapa'a, Hawaii. Guide books vaguely mention it and tourists cannot pronounce the name. *Rainbows Over Kapa'a* tells the story of Bill Fernandez and his Euro-Hawaiian family's 150 year history. The Fernandez-Scharsch family's struggle to survive and thrive in Kapa'a are poignantly chronicled in these pages.

During World War I, W.A. Fernandez, the son of a Hawaiian and an immigrant whaler from the Azores who jumped ship in Lahaina, arrived in town with movie projection equipment strapped to his back. He introduced the immigrant plantation labor to the wonders of silent movies. There, he met Agnes Scharsch, a young Hawaiian-Alsatian woman. While he traveled to the Orient to show his films, Agnes saved her pineapple cannery earnings to buy their eventual home.

At a time when Hawaiians rarely owned land or ran businesses, W.A. and Agnes decided to build an ambitious project on land they purchased. In 1939, it opened and was the largest movie theater in the islands. The magic of the movies filled the town with its music, drawing people to its center. Movies came to life when the real Fighting 69th arrived shortly after Pearl Harbor; Bill learned the value of shining shoes and being a go-fer.

Bill Fernandez describes his island childhood in this town built on marshlands and one of the few not owned by the sugar plantations. There he enjoyed the ocean, surfing, swimming, spear fishing and exciting hukilau. Joining his 'local' friends in mock battles and making tin canoes, they learned the value of cooperation, and creativity, from the bottom up.

Set in the lush Garden Isle, it celebrates the community of hard working, industrious people of many nationalities who succeeded by sharing and cooperating with a spirit of aloha. Today, witnessing America's mixed race president from Hawaii, we learn the source of his value system. These same values Bill exemplifies having grown up in the islands.

With aloha in his heart, Bill dedicates these pages to the memory of his parents, W.A. and Agnes who taught him to work hard, get an excellent education and be proud of his Hawaiian heritage.

Dr. John Lydgate

Acknowledgments

There are many people who have made this book happen. Marie Fifield of the Kaua'i Historical Society provided a key impetus in my writing of this story. She loved my first attempt, a book called, *The Roxy*. For years, she urged me to re-publish it, since there was a dearth of material on Kapa'a. Marie has been extraordinary in getting me the pictures and information that I needed to write this book. John Lydgate pushed a redoing of the Roxy story since the family theater played such an integral part in the life of the town. His constant prodding forced me into several re-drafts to more significantly describe Kapa'a. Many thanks to Andy Bushnell who asked many questions, pointed me in the right historical direction, and gave me valuable insights. David Penhallow transcribed an oral history given by my aunt Beatrice Lovell. This provided valuable background material for the life of Joseph Scharsch and the early days of the family in Kilauea and Kapa'a. My kudos to President Randy Wichman and the Kaua'i Historical Society for their unstinting support of *Rainbows Over Kapa'a*.

Historical books are dependent on the elders, the people who lived through the tumultuous times that are written about. Thanks to family members, now deceased, who orally shared their memories of the past. Thank you, Alice Morgan Paik and Stanford Morgan, for searching a century of your memories and providing me with corroboration of what I have written.

Thank you, Linda Paik Moriarty, for helping me sort through the past and providing me with family pictures. Thank you, Kubota brothers, for sharing remembrances of the Okinawan Japanese who came to Hawai'i to work in the sugar fields, then started small businesses servicing Kapa'a. Thank you, Haven Kuboyama, for sharing remembrances of the "good days." Thank you, Mr. and Mrs. Don Pixler, newcomers to Kapa'a, for the hours spent answering questions about the town. Thank you to the half dozen other young people I spoke to about the Kapa'a of today.

Thank you Kaua'i Community College for use of their Garden Island Newspaper archives.

Books cannot be written without a terrific support staff. My special thanks to Tammi Andersland, Editor of *The Pacific Journal*. She is my print editor and has done all that is necessary for publication.

Without my son, Jon Fernandez, I could not have overcome the technical difficulties of recovering material from the *Roxy* book and using it in this re-issue. For days, he assisted me in editing the current story, assembling the pictures and solving the intricacies of Microsoft Word, and doing a web page, wfernandez.com.

Finally, hugs, kisses, and kudos to my wife, Judie. Her support, patience, understanding, authorship, editing, data collection, pictures, work ethic, prodding, enthusiasm, love of Kapa'a, love of history, and so many other factors have been the life blood of this book. Her photographs of Kapa'a and people have made the book special. Without her, this story would not be written.

I dedicate *Rainbows Over Kapa'a* to my parents and the woman I love.

There are others who have helped that I may have left out from this acknowledgment. There may be facts that I recite which others may disagree with. Whatever mistakes or failures there may be, it is my responsibility. Much of what I say is based on memories of happenings that occurred a long time ago.

William J. Fernandez

Table of Contents

Table of Contents

Prologue

For a century and sixty-three years, Hawai'i was a land of mystery and conjecture until one beautiful day, the sun rose and death came from the sky. It was a "day of infamy" that people would never forget and from that time, Hawai'i was no longer mysterious.

Rainbows Over Kapa'a is the story of my hometown on the island of Kaua'i. From its marshlands, a pluralistic society developed where races blended to mirror the rich homogeneous pattern of Hawai'i. Kapa'a is a place where anyone with energy and enterprise can succeed. Come swim with me to my island in the Pacific.

Isolation is the key feature of Hawai'i; a vast ocean separates the islands from the rest of the world. Its remoteness and mineral-poor geology ensured that early voyagers, who made it their home, would develop a Stone Age self sufficient subsistence society. Map makers in the Modern Age did not catalogue these islands until Captain James Cook in 1778 stumbled upon them. Once found, its native people were thrust into a resource rich world far advanced from their own.

For early Hawaiians, American and European nations brought new ideas like private property and capitalism. These concepts clashed with traditional values of sharing the land and its products. During the nineteenth century, the common Hawaiians became penniless squatters on the *'aina* (land) that they believed was a living thing that could not be owned by anyone.

In the nineteenth century, the Hawaiian race appeared doomed to extinction. Disease and improvidence decimated thousands of natives. It took new blood lines from over the seas to save the Hawaiian. I am thankful for those immigrants from Asia and Europe who came, mated and ensured our survival. There are over 200,000 of us who are of mixed blood and we are stronger, healthier, and wiser because of our Caucasian and Asiatic ancestors.

This story will detail the struggle of my Hawaiian parents to acquire land, build a movie theater, and succeed. For them, their pot of gold was found at the end of the rainbow in Kapa'a, Kaua'i. This unique town gave impoverished Hawaiians and foreigners imported to work in the sugar plantations, an opportunity to earn a decent living, educate their children, and live a better life.

History is the story of people and events that got us where we are today. To understand the story of my family and Kapa'a town, it is important to delve into the past and learn of the life and times of William Antonne Fernandez (1880-1949) and his wife Agnes Fernandez (1896-1979).

In the nineteenth century there were three critical foreign impacts on the Hawaiian people: the land division law, the sugar industry, and modern communications. It was a time when the communal structure and oral traditions collided with Western concepts of private land ownership, capitalism, and visual means of communication.

The Great *Mahele*

Persuaded to preserve the indigenous population by providing for private land ownership, Kamehameha III in 1848 set in motion laws which allowed individuals to own land. Of the 4.1 million acres in Hawai'i, one third would be set aside for the king, one third for the nobles and one third as government land to be acquired as private property. This momentous event was known as "The Great *Mahele*." The result was not as envisioned by the King. Instead of individual plots of land being farmed by Hawaiian families, land ownership became concentrated in the hands of an educated minority of people, who understood the significance of private property and the making of money. The native people, raised in a society where everything was shared, did not grasp these concepts, nor did they understand the legal process to secure land ownership. Prior to the overthrow of the Hawaiian kingdom in 1893, approximately 28,000 acres of government land were owned by Hawaiians. For them, the land division law was a disaster; overnight, most became squatters. The true enormity of the law would not be discovered by the ordinary Hawaiian until the 1970's, when land development mushroomed and Hawaiian squatters were dispossessed from land they had farmed for a century.

Some say it is unwise to condemn this division even though it concentrated land ownership into the hands of a few. From the *mahele* (division) there grew the only viable economy Hawai'i was to have in the nineteenth century: **sugar**. Cultivation of sugar increased Hawai'i's declining population and fostered the growth of small towns throughout the islands as thousands of laborers and wanderers came to Hawai'i to work on the plantations. Sugar shaped the politics of Hawai'i, eventually leading to the overthrow of the Hawaiian monarchy in 1893. Sugar led to annexation to the United States in 1898 and eventual statehood in 1959. Sugar dominated the entire life and livelihood of everyone in Hawai'i for seventy five years between 1875 and 1950.

From Oral Tradition to "Jurassic Park"

In today's time, when the vast majority of people are literate and able to receive and transmit knowledge, it may be difficult to understand why Hawaiians had trouble comprehending Western concepts and ideas. Hawaiians did not have a written language, nor were they particularly competent in communicating by use of the visual arts. Like the early Greeks of Homer's time, theirs was an oral tradition. Knowledge passed from generation to generation by word of mouth. Learning came from memorization of spoken words, not from books or pictures.

It was the missionaries who created the Hawaiian alphabet and a written Hawaiian language. Yet, this was not enough. Western ideas had to be translated into Hawaiian words to teach advanced concepts to the native population. Some of these concepts, land ownership and capitalism, were incompatible with Hawaiian values and traditions and difficult to define.

To grasp the problem this presented, analogize it to the early days of computer use by educated people. Many of us turned on the electric power to a computer only to view a C: prompt that refused to give us anything other than an "error" message. Unless one typed in the correct DOS command, the machine would not work. This error message was a constant reminder that the user was computer illiterate. To make the machine obey, a dictionary of DOS commands had to be memorized.

It was the development of pictures with words underneath which made the interface between the computer and the human, user-friendly. Today, we communicate electronically by clicking the mouse button on a picture or word. Icons and words brought us from the primitive days of computer ignorance to present day wide-spread internet use.

First generation Euro-Hawaiians and Asian-Hawaiians who understood English words, pictures, and their meanings were the interface between the pure Hawaiian, steeped in an oral tradition, and an educated world. Agnes and William Fernandez were two Euro-Hawaiians educated in English who grasped the concepts of land ownership and capitalism. With this knowledge, they would achieve their dream of a better life for themselves and their Hawaiian children.

In the chapters ahead, the story of my parents, the Roxy Theater and Kapa'a Town unfolds. William and Agnes grew up in a time when the majority of people owned little and lived a bare existence. It was a time when land was owned or controlled by a wealthy few. It was a time when opportunities for economic success for the common Hawaiian rarely existed.

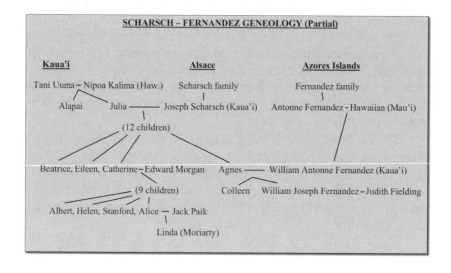

SCHARSCH – FERNANDEZ GENEOLOGY (Partial)

Kaua'i **Alsace** **Azores Islands**

Tani Uuma – Nipoa Kalima (Haw.)   Scharsch family   Fernandez family

Alapai   Julia ———— Joseph Scharsch (Kaua'i)   Antonne Fernandez - Hawaiian (Mau'i)

(12 children)

Beatrice, Eileen, Catherine – Edward Morgan   Agnes ——— William Antonne Fernandez (Kaua'i)

(9 children)   Colleen   William Joseph Fernandez – Judith Fielding

Albert, Helen, Stanford, Alice — Jack Paik

Linda (Moriarty)

Chapter 1

Pioneer Showman

An armada of 1,500 war canoes was assembled in 1796 on the northwest shore of O'ahu. Ten thousand warriors in their outriggers thrust themselves into the sixty mile channel separating O'ahu from Kaua'i. Within a few hours, the wind and currents capsized half of the canoes and Kamehameha ordered his remaining men to return to Waikiki. Six years later, the conqueror assembled a second mighty fleet of canoes and schooners. Many of his warriors were armed with muskets and his ships contained more than fifty cannon. Composing a *ho'ohiki*, a vow, Kamehameha promised his warriors that they would: "Drink of the sacred waters of Wailua, eat of the mullet of Kawaimakua and the *limu* of Polihale." Alas, typhoid fever struck his multitudes of fighting men, causing many to fall dead from the illness that turned bodies black. Frustrated by these disasters and angered by the refusal of the King of Kaua'i to surrender his island, Kamehameha hurled his war spear from O'ahu, piercing a hole into the top-most ridge of Anahola Mountain.

Like a Cyclops' gigantic eye, the hole-in-the-mountain looks down upon the northerly turning point in the belt trail that connects the habitable portions of the Garden Island. The trail begins at the cliffs of Polihale, winds along the coastline connecting the towns of Kekaha, Waimea, Hanapepe, Koloa, Lihu'e, Kapa'a, Kealia, Kilauea, and finally Hanalei on the north shore of Kaua'i. This trail continues past Hanalei into Ke'e Beach at Ha'ena where the rugged coastline forces it to narrow and rise, clinging to the steep edges of the volcanic Na Pali coastline, finally ending in mysterious Kalalau Valley, once populated by hundreds of Hawaiians.

From the point in the trail where the hole in Anahola Mountain can be seen, the coastline of Kaua'i changes. The beaches alter from soft sand to a rock-filled coastline as you continue north along the shore. The emerald green vegetation inland from the ocean holds promise that as you travel further north, the island and its jungles will take on a primitive dawn-of-creation look. Tall mountain peaks cloaked in soft clouds fade in and out of view like shy maidens; thin, silvery slivers of rain-fed waterfalls freefall down the steep volcanic mountains, often crowned with iridescent rainbows. Here, where the trail winds below the mountain, the land is sparsely populated. At the start of the twentieth century, only a handful of Hawaiians lived *kahakai*, along the shore.

In the early twentieth century, the hardened earth trail within sight of the hole-in-the-mountain weaved through lush green forests of kukui and koa trees draped with yam vines. It wound past misty glades of ferns and tropical shrubs that carpeted the rain-freshened earth. Decaying vegetation, disturbed by hooves or running feet, filled the air with its musty odor. Even though she played within this shadowy forest with other children from her *ohana* (family), young Agnes Scharsch feared this land beneath the glare of the Cyclops' eye because it was "*wao akua lapu,*" the jungle of the ghosts. Yet the mysterious soft darkness drew her into it where she could run along the trail, feeling the earth beneath her bare feet. Her light cotton dress shone like a bright flower against the deep greens of the ferns.

William Antonne Fernandez, in his dapper white suit astride his white horse, struck a handsome figure as he turned northward along the trail heading towards Kilauea town. His mount pulled a wagon loaded with his motion picture gear, projectors, hand cranked generator, film, a screen and other equipment necessary for showing silent movies. As he glanced up towards the hole-in-the-mountain, he wondered whether the eye of the Cyclops appreciated how splendid he appeared in his suit, tie and banded Panama hat.

Peering through the lacey, soft ferns beside the trail, Agnes' older brother Edward called to her, "*Akua lapu, hele mai!*" (Ghost coming, let's get out of here!) Startled, Agnes stared at the apparition slowly riding toward them. In her eyes, the figure in white was the boogie man and Agnes, who would one day marry William Antonne Fernandez, turned away from this spirit and ran screaming down the undulating bluffs towards grandpa's simple house on the beach at Moloa'a. Breathless, she told grandfather Tani about the ghost while he calmly stood knee-deep in the clear water fishing as his shark lazily swam past. "It's a terrifying *akua lapu* in the forest!" she said. For days, she did not venture forth from the safety of the seashore home of her Hawaiian grandfather.

W.A. Fernandez was not a ghost, but a pioneer showman of the Hawaiian Islands. Like the itinerant magic lantern projectionists of 19th century Europe, who traveled from village to village with their apparatus on their back, W.A. traveled from plantation town to plantation town in Hawai'i with his projector, film, and screen, showing silent movies. Finally, after years of wandering, W.A. met my mother Agnes, settled in Kapa'a and together they fulfilled his dream: the building of the Roxy Theater.

Chapter 2

Sugar is Power

Neolithic farmers in New Guinea first cultivated sugar cane 10,000 years ago. From that island, this member of the grass family spread to China, India, and into the Pacific. Polynesian colonizers brought sugar cane to Hawai'i. Although chewed by Hawaiians, it was not prized for its sweetness, but for its quick growth, bamboo-like strength, and dense foliage. These characteristics made it an excellent hedge and wind break. Native Hawaiians did not know methods of extraction of its juices necessary to create sugar.

Hawai'i, at the start of the nineteenth century, had a subsistence economy. Without natural resources, the new kingdom, established by Kamehameha the Great, had only food, water, and recreation to barter with foreign ships sailing the Pacific.

Traders found sandalwood growing in Hawaii and by 1810 a brisk trade ensued for this fragrant wood. Chinese prized it for its strong scent and used sandalwood in the making of furniture. Merchant sea captains negotiated with Hawaiian chiefs to buy the fragrant wood. These unscrupulous nobles impressed thousands of Hawaiian commoners into the backbreaking work of chopping down trees, hauling them from the mountains, and loading them onto waiting ships. Taro fields, fishing, and all forms of economic development or maintenance of villages were neglected. Within a few short years the inevitable result of this blind pursuit of money reaped its grim rewards: Hawaiians died by the thousands and the communal structure of Hawai'i was destroyed.

By 1830, the sandalwood industry was dead. Forests of sandalwood, indiscriminately cut down without any attempt at reforestation, were gone forever. Coupled with disease, sandalwood work had decimated the Hawaiians. Foolish and improvident chiefs had wiped out a potential long-term industry and a labor force. With the death of the sandalwood trade, Hawai'i had nothing of value to export and its subsistence economy was endangered. The monarchy needed a product to sell.

In 1802, Chinese adventurers on Lana'i, familiar with the making of sugar, experimented with the use of crude heavy granite rollers to crush the native plants. Their attempts to make molasses and then raw sugar crystals failed and efforts to make usable Hawaiian-grown sugar languished.

Despite the failure of the Lana'i experience, John Wilkinson in 1825, planted sugar cane in Manoa Valley on O'ahu. He distilled rum from the crushed cane. Hawai'i's Dowager Queen became so incensed by the drunkenness it brought, that she caused the still to be destroyed. Sugar cane growing for profit appeared ended for all time.

The isolated Hawaiian kingdom needed something to sell. Three enterprising young men from New England convinced Kamehameha III to grant them a royal patent for a thousand acres of land in Koloa, Kaua'i, for the cultivation of sugar cane. The locality was ideal for the industry, blessed with sunlit, arable land and an abundance of water. In 1835, Ladd & Company opened the first operative sugar mill in Hawai'i.

Sugar cane growing is labor intensive. Land must be cleared and tilled. Eighteen-inch cuttings are planted, irrigated for twenty two months, then starved of water for two months to send sweet juices to the stalks. Men must cut into the dense foliage to slice the bamboo-like cane and haul the cut stalks to wagons. In early plantation days, oxen pulled the wagons to the mill, but they had a limited working radius. This limitation reduced the amount of land that could profitably be worked to three miles from the sugar mill, the distance that animals could travel with a load in a workday. Because of this limitation and other factors, Ladd & Company failed; there was not enough growing area to provide for profitable production.

Alexander Liholiho, Kamehameha IV, on becoming king, was confronted with a monumental problem; his kingdom was destitute. Whaling, the economic mainstay of the kingdom after the demise of the sandalwood trade, was not providing sufficient income to fund the nation's needs. Adding to his problems, Hawaiians were dying at an alarming rate and, despite the land division law, very few were self sufficient.

Sugar, produced cheaply enough, could provide a viable economy, but entrepreneurs complained that there were not enough Hawaiians to work the fields. "We must have foreign laborers," argued the planters. "Hawaiians are too few and too lazy to do the hard work that sugar cane requires." Reluctantly, the King authorized the importation of foreign workers. The Chinese, hired at minimum wage for a three to five year contract, were the first to come to Hawai'i in 1852. Twenty five years later, Dr. William Hillebrand, a noted botanist, was appointed Commissioner of Immigration. He was responsible for bringing thousands of Portuguese and other Europeans to Hawaii.

Were there slaves who could have been used by the plantations? For centuries, Hawai'i had a slave class, the *kauwa*. They were the despicable ones, marked on the forehead with the slave sign. In ancient times, the *kauwa* were often used for human sacrifice. It is to the credit of the New England missionaries that the 1852 Hawaiian Constitution abolished slavery long before the American Civil War.

Cheap contract labor did not provide the answer to making the sugar mills profitable. Large quantities of sugar cane could not be produced by hand labor nor hauled to the mills by oxen. The steam engine made sugar cane growing economically viable. Once trains, steam plows, and advanced methods of extraction were introduced, investors came in droves to the islands to speculate in Hawaiian sugar since the yields per acre were higher than anywhere else.

New technology and cheap labor were still not enough. Hawaiian sugar needed to be shipped long distances to world markets. Countries, like the United States, had import taxes which marked up the price of sugar and reduced profits. Hawaiian sugar received a shot in the arm with the American Civil War. Sugar from southern states was embargoed by the North and prices leaped. Hawai'i's plantations became profitable and were able to expand. To meet the demand, more foreign labor was imported and new equipment purchased. A few men became rich.

When the Civil War ended, sugar prices fell. Hawaiian business interests faced a crisis. While they had cheap labor and land, transportation costs and import taxes eliminated profits. For several years, plantations stagnated and labor importation slowed. The sugar owners begged the monarchy to secure a reciprocity treaty with the United States. Such a treaty would allow Hawaiian products to be imported into America duty free.

There were two major stumbling blocks to a reciprocity treaty. One was the United States Senate that did not condone the indentured servitude of foreign laborers who worked in the sugar fields. These men were paid a pittance wage of three dollars per month and flogged if they did not work. The second was Kamehameha V, Lot, King of Hawai'i from 1863 to 1872. He was opposed to such a treaty since it might mean annexation to America or a surrender of control over Pearl Harbor, the most important naval port in the Pacific.

When Lot died without naming a successor, political tensions ran high in Honolulu. The Constitution provided that the legislature would select the new king. The sugar people backed William Lunalilo, and he was elected. Before he could secure a reciprocity treaty for the plantations, he died on February 3, 1874.

The popular choice of the Hawaiians for the new monarch was Dowager Queen Emma. She did not favor reciprocity or the loss of Pearl Harbor. The only other candidate was David Kalakaua who was a distant relative of King Kamehameha I and a member of the House of Nobles. As a legislator he had been outspokenly anti-American and an opponent of reciprocity.

On the eve of the election, there was talk of revolution. British and United States warships in Honolulu Harbor were prepared to land marines for the protection of lives and property. To the chagrin of many Hawaiians, Kalakaua made a deal with the plantation owners, promising to secure a reciprocity treaty if they would back his candidacy.

When Kalakaua was elected king by a plantation controlled assembly, Hawaiians rioted. One legislator was killed and others injured. Violence stopped when foreign troops landed and brought order to the capitol. After Kalakaua ascended the throne, he fulfilled his campaign promise by traveling to Washington D.C. and securing a reciprocity treaty from the U.S. Senate. President Ulysses S. Grant signed it in 1876.

The result of reciprocity was astounding. In 1875, there were twenty sugar mills in Hawai'i. By 1880, there were sixty three. Overnight, thousands of acres of land were converted into sugar plantations. The importation of foreign laborers accelerated and soon plantation towns mushroomed throughout the Hawaiian Islands.

The wealth brought on by sugar profits produced a two-tier society: the rich few, and the many landless foreign laborers and Hawaiians. The imported workers and the indigenous people were uneducated, poor, and without prospects for a better life. Their lives were controlled by a small group of wealthy men.

Chapter 3

Kapa'a: Rainbow Community of Opportunity

Wai'ale'ale Mountain dominates Kaua'i. Six million years ago, this five thousand foot shield volcano created the oldest of the Hawaiian Islands. Its name is derived from the rippling pond that cradles in the hollow of its summit. At one edge of the pond, overlooking the Wailua River, is a lava rock altar to the Hawaiian God Kane. During ancient times, royalty and their retainers made an annual trek along the banks of the river and up the slope to the top of the mountain. There, they worshipped and made sacrifices to the God.

This dead volcano is the wettest spot on earth with an average annual rainfall of four hundred and thirty inches descending on its summit. Its pond supplies fresh water to several of the rivers and streams of Kaua'i. These waterways serve as long-distance sieves, transporting and depositing rocks, pebbles, and finer sediments as they move towards the sea. When descending fresh water strikes the heavier volume of ocean water, it overflows onto flatlands, depositing rich soils onto them. These enriched wetlands are ideal ground for the growing of rice.

Rice has fed the greatest number of people for a longer period of time than any other crop. It is first mentioned in Chinese chronicles in 3,000 B.C., as the most important of the five food plants. Rice is hardy; its efficient ecological system of air passage from roots to shoots means it can be grown effectively in water-logged soils. Most rice is produced when grown in the silt soils created where major rivers emerge from hills and mountains. Water washing over lava rocks produces these soils, full of nutrients needed for successful rice production.

When Captain James Cook arrived at Kaua'i, the heavily populated areas of the island were Koloa, Waimea, Wailua, Hanalei, and Kalalau. Kapa'a, meaning "the solid," is not mentioned in early histories.

There is an ancient legend that relates the story of a giant emerging from the sea, demanding of the people of Kapa'a food to satisfy his hunger. Fearful of the power of this monster, they brought him what they had. Yet the elders knew that before long, the swine and fowl would be gone and the giant would consume the common folk. They concocted a brew that would put the mighty man to sleep forever. The giant drank the potion, yawned, and lay down to rest with his head by a waterfall and his feet stretching toward the Anahola Mountains. Soon grass and trees sprouted over him; his body became one with the earth and his sleep became eternal.

The legend of Sleeping Giant Mountain may not be proof that Hawaiians once lived in the area of Kapa'a, but the mountain's presence and height are significant. Clouds, heavy with moisture, flowing inland from the sea, must rise over it. As they climb, heavy rain falls. This rain water is trapped in the flatlands creating marshes. Historically, during heavy rains, the marshland has overflowed and flooded Kapa'a. This periodic flooding of the marshland must have made the area an undesirable place for Hawaiians to live.

My home town is never mentioned in early histories as having a thriving Hawaiian village. Other than an occasional archeological find, there are no signs of ancient habitation in the vicinity: no taro terraces, rock walls, canals, fish ponds, or stone temples. As a child digging into the sand dunes fringing Kapa'a, I would uncover an occasional human bone, but never an ancient artifact. Contrast this with Po'ipu on the south end of the island, where thousands of human remains have been uncovered, or the area of Wailua River where ancient temples can still be found. Given the dearth of pre-contact human habitation, why did Kapa'a become the center of the most populous district of the island of Kaua'i?

The development of Kapa'a was caused by its marshes. The area had ideal conditions for growing rice: sun-drenched, swampy land enriched by silt-filled soils. When thousands of Chinese laborers were imported to work in the sugar fields of Hawai'i and the railroads in California, it was inevitable that they would demand rice. This was the impetus for rice growing on Kaua'i.

Enterprising Chinese, on completing their labor contracts, sought out cheap, wet, land to grow rice. Commercial rice growing began in Hanalei and spread to the marsh-filled land of Kapa'a. *Pake* (Chinese) men diked the area, built shanties and began planting rice. This haphazard settlement of *Pake* would not be enough to make a windswept flood plain grow into a viable town. Sugar and a king would be its catalyst for growth.

Fresh from his success in putting together a reciprocity treaty with the U.S. Congress, King David Kalakaua took advantage of the profit opportunities that reciprocity provided by convincing several investors to form the Makee Sugar Company. In April 1877, the company leased 13,400 acres of government land, between Kapa'a and Anahola, for $600 a year and built a sugar mill at Kealia.

With a group of his court followers, Kalakaua then formed the "*Hui Kawaihau*" to grow sugar cane for Makee. Kalakaua and his retinue came to Kapa'a accompanied by an experienced sugar planter, James Makee. They built a sugar mill, housing, and a meeting hall for the King's courtiers.

Yet court followers are not smart farmers. The functionaries had little knowledge of growing and processing sugar. Profits were poor and when James Makee died, the venture failed. The Kapa'a mill was dismantled and moved to Kealia. The buildings built by the *Hui* (club) were vacated. Kapa'a appeared doomed to be a backwater habitat of isolated squatter shanties of expatriate Chinese laborers.

Chapter 4

19th Century European Adventurers

"Oh, I'm a Portuguese whaler," crooned Don Ho, "far away from home." The nighttime crowd at Duke's went wild as my classmate from Kamehameha Schools wailed out the story of a lonely sailor from the Azores seeking love in Hawai'i. For forty years, Ho was one of the premier entertainers in Hawai'i. But few people know of his disastrous debut in California. Before he became famous, Don and I were in summer camp at Mather Air Force base in Sacramento. We were invited to a bar to sing Hawaiian songs for our dinner. We sang off key and were never fed.

Whales are the largest creatures on earth. A fully-grown blue whale weighs in excess of two hundred tons and will achieve a length of 100 feet. These mammals are migratory, preferring the Arctic waters to hunt their favorite food, tiny shrimp called krill, and, for breeding, the warm tropical waters of Hawai'i. Whales, dolphins, and porpoises form a group of mammals called cetaceans. They are docile, even friendly, until harpooned.

European whaling began in the twelfth century with the Basques who pursued the mammals in the Bay of Biscay. When the bay was fished out, fishermen moved further into the Atlantic. Whaling was a profitable business due to the variety of salable items that can be made from the carcasses. Oil from whale blubber was used for light, margarine, paint, lubricants, and soap. From the animal's baleen came umbrellas, skirt hoops, corset stays, and fabric stiffeners. Its ribs provided scrimshaw jewelry, its intestines amber gris used in the manufacture of expensive perfumes.

By the early nineteenth century, whales were sparse in the Atlantic, but demand for whale products had grown and the Pacific had many whales. Fleets of whaling ships descended on Hawai'i to spear the mammals breeding in its warm tropic waters, or used the islands as a rest stop before pursuing them into the Arctic. There were two ideal

ぞ

ports for the ships to anchor, Lahaina and Fair Haven, known today as Honolulu.

In ancient times, Lahaina, Mau'i, was a dusty, squalid seaside village of shacks flung up in piecemeal fashion. Mountain ranges to the east robbed Lahaina of rainfall leaving the hills above the village rocky and barren. The western sun baked the area with a fiery heat giving Lahaina its name: merciless sun. The features that made it desirable for whalers were its broad sand beaches, calm water, and a protected anchorage.

In 1819, the year of Kamehameha's death and the overthrow of the *kapu* system, whalers from New England came to Lahaina for water and food. What they also found were alcohol and women. Word soon spread and whaling ships began to arrive by the hundreds. Lahaina was an ideal place to resupply and provide sailors a much-needed rest before heading into Arctic waters.

For fifty years, whaling meant wealth for Hawai'i. Resident merchants supplied goods to refit ships and transshipped whale products to Atlantic ports; local farmers provided whalers with food. Along the waterfront of Lahaina and Honolulu, there grew a multitude of shops, saloons, and whore houses. Among the whalers who came to Lahaina to rest, get drunk, and womanize were Portuguese seamen from the Azores.

In the Atlantic, there are nine islands of volcanic origin forming the archipelago of the Azores. These islands are the nipples of volcanoes which are part of the Mid-Atlantic Chain. This range of mountains rises above the surface of the ocean at the Azores and then stretches underwater to surface again at Iceland. The geological creation of the Azorean Archipelago is the same as the Hawaiian; they were formed by tectonic plates gliding over the earth. At various points there are "hot spots" fixed in place. As a tectonic plate inches over a "hot spot," burning magma spouts out of the earth's crust through a seam in the plate. The result is a chain of islands like Hawai'i and the Azores.

Discovered in the fifteenth century and populated by Flemings and Portuguese, the Azores are subject to the nation of Portugal, a thousand miles to the east. During the days of the Conquistadors, it was a natural stopping place for the gold-laden ships traveling from the New World to Spain. It is a superb area for fishing. The mid-Atlantic chain, emerging from the depths of the ocean at the Azores, forms a shallow escarpment from which volcanoes rise above the sea. Along this escarpment, fish and seafood abound. One half of all the world's game fishing records have been set in these waters.

In olden times, whales fed in great numbers near the nine volcanic islands. Herds of blue whales just beneath the surface of the sea gobbled up great schools of plankton, while thousands of sperm whales sounded as much as a mile in pursuit of squid. With a multitude of these sea mammals feeding along the escarpment, it was inevitable that inhabitants of the nine islands became whalers. Beginning in May, farmers would search from their *"gigias,"* cliff-top watchtowers, for the coming of the whales. The sight of the first spouts signaled the seasonal arrival of the mammals and the watchers rang bells to alert the town. With this announcement, farmers became fishermen, running to their narrow, tippy, wooden boats and oaring out to sea to hunt. For hundreds of years, Azoreans fished in the same way. They contested with the cetaceans in man-powered rowing boats, using puny metal spears attached to rope. They engaged these monsters in a contest evenly pitting man against beast. Sometimes the beast won.

Born on one of the nine islands, Antonne Fernandez was a typical Azorean, a farmer and a fisherman. He was built like a gorilla, barrel chested, very strong, and bald. Unwillingly, he became a whaler, either due to impressment on a whaling boat or a decision to leave the Azores because of its poor economy. Although his reasons for departing from his homeland are unclear, what is certain is that once at sea, he did not enjoy the rigorous life of whaling.

We know from books like *Moby Dick*, that life was hazardous for whalers. The animals might turn on their tormentors, overturning their puny boats. Flensing, the slicing of a whale for its blubber, was done at sea. A whaler stood on roped planks just above the floating carcass and cut it into sections. While he worked, sharks, attracted by blood, tore chunks from the animal. Waves constantly rocked the boat. If a man fell, he would be eaten or frozen in moments.

No one in the family knows the reasons for Antonne's desertion from his whaling ship. We do know that there was a huge Arctic freeze in 1871 that destroyed more than forty ships and doomed whaling in the Pacific. We also know that there were many dark-skinned beauties in Lahaina, who preferred the company of a Caucasian to that of a Hawaiian. Without permission, Fernandez jumped ship. He married a pure Hawaiian, then another, and again another. From one of these unions, William Antonne Fernandez was born in 1880.

At birth, W. A. was *hanai* (adopted) to his Hawaiian grandmother. This was a common practice in early Hawai'i. It is claimed that its purpose was to provide loving care with an extended family. Probably closer to the truth was economics. All Hawaiian families, except royalty, were poor; many children living under one roof led to scarcity of food for all. Spreading them around to relatives, friends, even strangers, meant survival for them and the families from which they came. Yet there was a cost to this practice, the loss of the love of a father and mother. King Kalakaua was haunted by being *hanai*. William Antonne Fernandez never mentioned or talked about his mother; it was as if she never existed. His father was mentioned, but always with respect.

During the time that William grew up with his grandmother (*tutu*), his father worked as a *paniolo* (cowboy) at the Parker Ranch on the island of Hawai'i. The care and education of his son was left to *tutu*. As a result, William's first language was Hawaiian and he was trained to think and be Hawaiian. This knowledge would be helpful in later life and yet prove a source of pain for him as well.

At the age of eight, with rudimentary schooling, William was summoned to the Parker Ranch to be its mail carrier, traveling from the ranch at Mauna Kea to Hilo and back, a thirty mile round trip. The young boy became a pony express rider and for seven years transported mail. Later, he would say about his work, "Mail carrier, *paniolo*, jack of all trades, master of none."

Although he loved the high mountain climate of Mauna Kea, William believed his father was too harsh. He explained this by describing the story of the horse that would not move. "My father tugged on its reins once, then twice. On the third pull without any sign of movement, he turned and hit the horse along the jaw with a right hook. The horse was felled to the ground by the force of the blow."

At fifteen, William fled. He left for a mix of reasons: the harshness of his parent who believed that, "the only good boy was a hard working boy," and the lure of the big city of Honolulu. He left at a time when a revolution had occurred in Hawai'i. Queen Lili'uokalani had been deposed, a republic had replaced the monarchy, and the queen languished in prison, charged by the Republic of Hawai'i with the crimes of treason and sedition.

Meanwhile, another European came to the islands to work in the newly developing sugar fields of Kaua'i. This wanderer would marry Julia Uuma and, from this union, produce a daughter named Agnes Scharsch, William's future wife.

While Hawai'i's sugar plantations were seeking a reciprocity treaty, in Europe, Otto von Bismarck, Chancellor of Prussia, proceeded to create a German Empire by pursuing limited wars. To this end, the Prussian army defeated Denmark in 1864 and then beat the Austro-Hungarian Empire in 1866. Next, Bismarck manipulated a war with France to recover lost German lands, Alsace-Lorraine.

These two provinces are located west of the Rhine River, in the foothills of the Swiss Alps. They have been a battleground between the German and Gallic tribes of Western Europe for many years. During the eighteenth century, France seized both regions from weak Germanic states bordering the Rhine.

In 1870, Bismarck convinced the Prussian Kaiser, Wilhelm I, that the acquisition of the provinces would be the final step in the creation of a German Empire. Blinded by his ego, Emperor Napoleon the III was maneuvered into war with Prussia. In six weeks, the army of France was destroyed. Paris was placed under siege by the Prussians and surrendered in January of 1871. The peace treaty that followed ceded the homeland of Joseph Scharsch, Alsace, to the German Empire.

The province of Alsace is unusual for it has aspects of three nations in its people, culture, and customs: Switzerland, Germany, and France. Its citizens are taller and more robust than the average Frenchman, and are fluent in French and German. Strasbourg is Alsace's largest city and its leading industrial center.

Joseph Scharsch grew up near Strasbourg. He was a member of a prominent Catholic family; two of his relatives were priests in the Church. The Scharsch family operated a restaurant and winery near the Rhine River where Joseph trained as a cook and vintner.

Once the treaty of peace with France was concluded, Germany instituted military conscription in the sister provinces. Young Scharsch was twenty years old and of prime military age. Threatened with being drafted, he decided not to serve in the army of the Kaiser, and announced to his parents that he would leave for America.

Joseph fled Alsace and worked his way across the Atlantic to the United States. There he found odd jobs, serving as a roust-about, waiter, cook, anything that paid money. He must have thought the Kaiser had an exceedingly long arm since he kept moving west, finally arriving in San Francisco. He worked as a cook for a period of time until he raised the money for passage to Honolulu. Here was a haven so far from the Kaiser that even the efficient Prussian military machine would never find him.

In the nineteenth century, work on the sugar plantations was labor intensive. Hand cutting of stalks was the method of harvesting cane. Once separated from the earth, they were put into wagons and hauled to the nearest mill. There, the cane was unloaded, ground into syrup, and the raw sugar separated from the liquid. These sweet brown crystals were bagged, drayed to a dock, and manhandled onto small boats that took them to a freighter for shipment to the United States.

Very few of the polyglot of contract laborers were skilled or understood English. They required intensive supervision. Plantation managers believed that educated Caucasians were needed to direct them.

In Honolulu, Joseph Scharsch found employment as a hotel cook, until he learned that Kilauea Sugar Company was looking for Caucasian men to serve as *luna*, field supervisors. He applied, was hired, and came to Kaua'i in the late 1870's.

For working men, there were few choices for female companionship. Hawaiian women were the only ones available. In the two-tiered society of the rich and the poor folk, it was unheard of for a white woman to associate with a man who was not Anglo-Saxon.

For a mate, Joseph Scharsch had only Hawaiians to choose from. Caucasian women of marriageable age were not available to him, as he was not of the correct class of Caucasian, being a field supervisor and not of proper breeding. On the other hand, a Hawaiian family wanted their daughters to marry Europeans. A field *luna* was a huge movement up the economic ladder for a landless native woman.

While serving as a cook at the Hawaiian Hotel in Honolulu, Joe had met a man named Titcomb. They became good friends. Titcomb owned property in Kilauea and when he heard Scharsch wanted to marry, he arranged with forty Hawaiian families to each bring a daughter to a meeting shack. Tani Uuma, a fisherman, and friend of Scharsch, brought his daughter, Julia, to the gathering.

In the middle of the building, Joseph sat surrounded by forty brown, teen-aged beauties. Outside, mothers and fathers waited for his selection. Scharsch surveyed the crowd and heard a giggle. He looked and saw a girl dodging behind another. He surveyed the room again and heard another giggle. Stalking over to the noise maker, Joseph saw Julia hiding behind several young women.

"Why are you laughing?" he demanded.

"Because you so funny looking, when searching for a wife."

"Why are you hiding?"

"My father told me to hide so you wouldn't pick me."

"Well, I am picking you," said Joseph.

"No," wailed the unhappy girl, "pick someone else, you got plenty to choose from."

Julia was 4 feet 11 inches tall and slight of build. She first had a good look at her future husband as she stood beside the priest on her wedding day, three days later. Joseph Scharsch was a true Alsatian, six feet, six inches in height. He was light skinned and the tallest man Julia had ever seen. She wailed and burst into tears, crying throughout the ceremony, barely able to repeat her vows through the sobs. Yet it is said by the family that, once the wedding was concluded, Julia ruled Joseph with an iron hand.

For a time, Scharsch continued to work for Kilauea Sugar Plantation and raise his family on a farm he had acquired in Kilauea. Unlike the Hawaiian, who was usually landless and without money, Scharsch was a knowledgeable European. He understood that ownership of land meant status and a means of making money grow. Although his wages were less than a dollar a day, he had saved his pennies and purchased property to build a home in Kilauea.

After many years of farming, Joe discovered that plantations are heartless. He had bought five acres from a Hawaiian who had dug a ditch to the Kilauea River to secure water. Scharsch continued using the ditch, but eventually discovered that the plantation claimed ownership of the land adjacent to the river. His access to water was shut off and the manager offered a pittance for Joe's property. When he refused the offer, Joe was fired. Several years of litigation followed. He won his case for water rights before a Kaua'i jury, but lost in the Hawai'i Supreme Court.

At the time the case was being considered, Makee Sugar Company in Kealia was prospering. Laborers were pouring into the area. Workers' camps had been built in Kealia and Kapa'a. Demand for rice was slowing and the Chinese rice farmers had become merchants, opening shops in Kapa'a town and selling goods to the plantation workers.

Scharsch took a job with Makee and moved his family to Kapa'a. It was a momentous moment when a Caucasian and his Hawaiian wife integrated the town. The wealthy plantation families lived in enclaves in the south and west end of the island, separating themselves from the laborers and Hawaiians. For the first time in Kapa'a, a Northern European moved in with the poor and the people of color.

Kapa'a was not a typical plantation town, founded and controlled by the sugar owners for the sole purpose of fueling the mill with workers. Instead, it had its own unique identity where people of many races lived and owned businesses. Why was this so? The answer is that the plantation owners did not want it and land was available and affordable. Everyone who lived in the town started life impoverished. They knew the value of working hard and together. In Kapa'a, immigrants, who had been subjugated in the past, found freedom to develop their properties and raise families without interference from a higher authority. As Spock on the Starship Enterprise would say, in Kapa'a you could live a long life and prosper.

Chapter 5

A Mounted Policeman

"Manuela boy, my dear boy, you no moah hila hila. No more fi'
cents no moah house go aala paki hia moe," was the jaunty song that
Hilo Hattie sang so saucily with Harry Owens. This ditty describes a
poor boy, Manuela, who has no money, no shame, "*hila hila*," and no
house; all he has is the park to sleep in. This song described William
Antonne Fernandez's status as a penniless fifteen year old when he
arrived in Honolulu in 1895. It was a time when momentous political
changes had occurred in Hawai'i.

"King David Kalakaua was profligate and pretentious," said the
Hawaiian League. He was pretentious in his grandiose design of
uniting the Polynesian Pacific islands into one empire under his
leadership. He was profligate by spending away the Hawaiian treasury
building a mini-European palace in the middle of Honolulu, having an
expensive coronation, and in illegally selling an opium license.

Members of the Hawaiian League, composed of missionary
families and Caucasian business men, armed themselves with rifles and
bayonets. In June of 1887, the League coerced Kalakaua into a new
constitution. This constitution stripped him of all power and placed the
supervision of the monarchy in the hands of a cabinet of ministers
composed of members of the League. Significantly, the new
constitution eliminated landless Hawaiians from voting for members of
the House of Nobles and disenfranchised most Orientals. The
Hawaiians call it the "Bayonet Constitution," because of the show of
force used in creating it.

One dramatic moment occurred during the takeover of the
kingdom. Armed members of the League invaded the home of Walter
Murray Gibson, the king's prime minister. The League hated Gibson,
for he was outspoken in his demands that, "Hawai'i should be for the
Hawaiians and governed by Hawaiians." Gibson and his son-in-law
were seized by armed men and ushered to the docks where they were
to be hung. Only the intervention of the British minister to Hawai'i
saved them from hanging.

King Kalakaua died in San Francisco, on January 20, 1891. Despite being just a puppet king after the implementation of the Bayonet Constitution, he had one last card to play: the right to choose a successor. Hawai'i's Merry Monarch, friend of Robert Louis Stevenson, chose as the ruler to succeed him his sister, Lili'uokalani.

Although told to obediently let her ministers run the government, Lili'uokalani on becoming queen attempted to promulgate Gibson's policies, by eliminating the Bayonet Constitution and returning Hawaii to the control of the Hawaiian people. She prepared a new Constitution to this effect. News of her actions enraged the businessmen of Honolulu. Incited by members of the Hawaiian League, and using the pretext of danger to American lives and property, United States Minister John L. Stevens ordered American Marines to march on 'Iolani Palace and aid in deposing the Queen. It was January 17, 1893, when Queen Lili'uokalani surrendered to "the superior power of the United States." Throwing herself on the mercy of the American people, she left the palace and ordered Hawaiians not to resist.

Members of the Hawaiian League rushed to Washington to secure annexation. After investigating the circumstances, President Grover Cleveland rebuffed them and admonished Congress that: "The claimed revolution and overthrow of the monarchy had not occurred by either popular revolution or suffrage, (but by) the lawless occupation of Honolulu under false pretexts by the United States." Upon the rejection of annexation by Congress, the League members, thirteen in number, declared Hawai'i a Republic. Sanford B. Dole, of missionary family and educated on Kaua'i, was named its first President.

At the time W.A. Fernandez arrived in Honolulu, the Republic was in turmoil. A counter-revolutionary plot had been uncovered and insurgents were captured and on trial. Queen Lili'uokalani was imprisoned, charged with high treason for allegedly instigating the revolt. While in prison, she composed many songs, including the sad and poignant "*Aloha Oe.*"

In Honolulu, W.A. Fernandez took any job available: bartender, racehorse jockey, janitor, anything paying money. Most important, W.A. went to school to get an education. He believed that the worth of a man could be found in the perfection of his penmanship, his ability to spell, to add and subtract, and his unflinching honesty.

In 1898, William McKinley succeeded Grover Cleveland as President of the U.S. and war with Spain followed. The American Asiatic Fleet sailed into Spanish-controlled Manila Bay in the Philippines, sinking a Spanish naval force. From these activities, it became clear that if the United States was to be a great power in the Pacific, Pearl Harbor must belong to it. McKinley knew that the U. S. Senate would never approve of annexation by the two-thirds vote required. Through an adroit parliamentary maneuver, he presented the treaty of annexation as a joint resolution to be adopted by majority vote in both houses of Congress. The Newlands Resolution was passed and Hawai'i was annexed. In 1900, Congress enacted an Organic Act creating the Territory of Hawai'i. McKinley appointed Sanford B. Dole as its first Governor.

Within a few years, a conservative "Big Five" dominated legislature controlled the territory. Many Hawaiians disagreed with annexation. There were petitions and protests against the loss of Hawaiian independence. A constabulary was needed. W.A. could ride a horse. He was intelligent and spoke Hawaiian fluently. Issued a badge and a gun, he became a police officer for the Ewa district of O'ahu and then a mounted patrolman in Honolulu. His assignment: keep the territorial peace.

Agnes Scharsch   William Fernandez

Jilted by his first wife, my dad proposed marriage to my mother in 1921.
She insisted that he take his movies to the Orient and think it over.

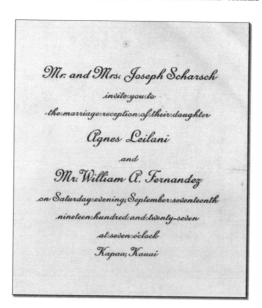

Dad returned to Kaua'i, proposed again and wedding bells.

My dad sailed on this ship to Japan. For 4 years he showed his movies in the Orient.

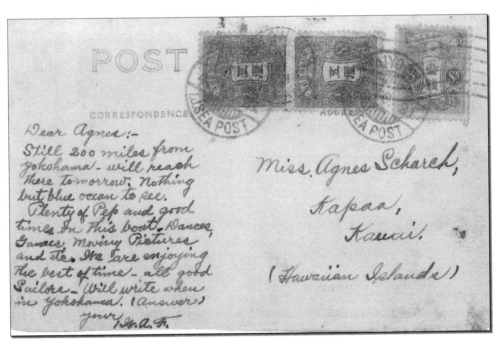

Great Grandfather Tani Uuma and his wife, Nipoa Kalima, both pure Hawaiians. He came to Kaua'i by canoe from Hana, Maui and Nipoa by canoe from Kohala, Hawai'i. They married and settled in Koo'lau, Kaua'i.

Family of Joseph Scharsch in Alsace, Germany. Father Scharsch on left and mother on right. Photo was taken prior to the Franco-Prussian War of 1870.

Julia Uuma in her wedding dress. At fourteen, Joseph Scharsch picked her from a bevy of 40 young Hawaiian girls. They married 3 days later.

Wedding luau for Joseph Scharsch and Julia Uuma, 1879. This matrimonial celebration lasted three days. "Kani kapila," all made happy music.

Great Uncle Alapai, brother of Grandmother, Julia Uuma

Joseph Scharsch seated with fifth child, Edward, in 1894. Julia is on the left, the other woman is unknown. The couple would have 12 children.

Nipoa Kalima Uuma with Morgan grandchildren. From the left: Alice, Edward, Elaine, and Arthur. 1917 photo.

Tani Uuma with grandchildren.

Grandparents, Julia and Joseph Scharsch, surrounded by their family: sons, daughters and grandchildren. They created a diverse legacy. 1923 photo.

Catherine Scharsch Morgan (Auntie Katie) at family home, Kapa'a.

The house I lived in as a child for 3 years. The breadfruit (ulu) tree I climbed to sing
Over the Rainbow.

Aunt Catherine Scharsch Morgan wearing a dozen strands of Ni'ihau shell lei. Katie was an authority on Hawaiian quilts, famous for her weaving and feather lei making.

Born in New York, Edward Joseph Morgan came to Kapa'a at the turn of the century to work for Makee as a construction engineer. He married Catherine Scharsch and had nine children. His sister, Margaret, was the wife of Hawaii Governor, Charles James McCarthy.

Railroad car used as transport to Makee in Kealia. Commuting to work in the late 19th century, Morgan gets an early start before the Kapa'a traffic builds. In background, the marshlands and rice fields. The tracks ran parallel to the Scharsch and Morgan homes.

Aunt Beatrice Scharsch Lovell, married to Sheriff Enoka Lovell of Lihue. Past President of Kaua'i Chapter Ka'ahumanu Society. Aunt Bea recorded an oral history of her family that is documented in the archives of the Kaua'i Historical Society.

Helen Morgan Rodrigues, Joseph Rodrigues, (aka John Dillinger) Margaret
Scharsch Hamamoto, Catherine Scharsch Morgan.

This photo was taken around 1944. Happy times when Auntie Eileen returned to
Kaua'i from Atlanta, Georgia, with her children.

Chapter 6

Words Come Alive

Epic poets like Homer and Pindar painted images of heroes and legendary events with their eloquent words. Eager audiences transformed their words into mental pictures of action. These epics, recounting past historical events, became legends, re-told down through the millennia. Artists over the centuries transferred the poetry of the Iliad and Odyssey into pictures on stone and canvas.

Likewise in ancient Hawai'i, people passed news of significant events from one person to the other by the "coconut wireless." For example, the news of the demise of Captain Cook was transmitted orally throughout the island of Hawai'i within a day of his death. News from the world outside of Hawai'i took months to arrive, because all communication from other countries came to the islands by ship.

It was a fleet that was sent to die that drew Hawai'i and the world together. During the Russo-Japanese War, the Tsar ordered his navy to sail from its ports on the Baltic to the Sea of Japan. Its movement, as it cruised half way around the world, was reported by means of the telegraph. Because of these instantaneous wireless communications, everyone knew of the fleet's progress as it sailed toward Korea. Steaming into the Straits of Tsushima in 1905, the iron ships of Russia were met by a newly commissioned fleet of the nation of Japan. Like Lord Nelson at Trafalgar, Admiral Togo achieved the classical naval maneuver of "crossing the T," and annihilated the Russian fleet.

Fluttering from the bow of the admiral's command ship was the flag of the new Empire of Japan depicting a blazing red, rising sun. Serving on Togo's flagship was future Grand Admiral Isoroku Yamamoto. He preserved this flag and, 36 years later, presented it to the aviators of Japan before their attack on Pearl Harbor. Inspired by it, they bombed the sleeping American fleet and achieved for the Empire its second great naval victory in the Pacific.

A newly installed transatlantic cable brought the news of Tsushima straits to Hawai'i and W.A. Fernandez. Thirsting for information about the momentous events occurring in the outside world, local businessmen and the literate curious crowded the telegraph office in Honolulu to read the ticker tape. But it was not news of naval victories like Tsushima Straits that excited the men of downtown Honolulu, it was boxing. Four decades after the fight, W.A. could recount, word-for-word, the ticker tape recitation of the championship battle between James Jeffries and Jack Munroe occurring in far away San Francisco, California.

In his verbal re-creation of the heavyweight fight recited to me as a child, he painted the scene at the Western Union office in Honolulu. *Hundreds of men thronged the agency and overflowed onto the street outside. The telegraphed news from San Francisco was relayed by word of mouth as the ticker tape printed out the electronic messages. "Jeffries enters the ring, and Jack Munroe is cowering in his corner," W.A. recited from memory that long-gone day. He described, in word and pantomime, how the assembled crowd at the Western Union office roared in derision of Munroe's fright. The Western Union wires fell silent for many minutes, and so did W.A. Suddenly, he became galvanized when the electronic messages clicked into action, and Munroe made a fight of it, bloodying Jeffries' face. But in the second round, "The champion threw a left hook to the body," Fernandez recounted as he stood up to demonstrate the powerful blow, "and then an uppercut to the chin. Munroe is down for the count," my dad shouted, swinging his arms to illustrate the actions of the heavy weight champion. "The crowd at the Western Union station went wild," yelled dad, as he hypnotically relived an event that occurred on August 26, 1904.*

Several years before the heavyweight championship fight, W.A. had reconciled with his father and the two men had gone into the stage coach business. When that venture failed, they became fish mongers. While catching *moi* (king fish) from a rocky promontory, Antonne Fernandez was smashed into boulders by a giant wave. He was hit again by another wave and, with water swirling around him, was pulled into the sea. Unfortunately, Portuguese whaler Fernandez had never learned to swim. He drowned and his body was not recovered.

This tragedy ended my dad's fishing enterprise. From that time on, he would not enter the sea. The memory of his father's abrupt death haunted him. There was another reason to quit, "we were always broke," he said. That was why he chose law enforcement; it was "a steady job with steady pay."

At the time of the fight, W.A. was serving as a Honolulu policeman. Believing he could not advance in life by remaining a law man, he took a job with the Honolulu Transit Company. In his spare time, he educated himself by taking correspondence courses in business management and public speaking. After two years of collecting tram tickets, W.A. went into business and, like Harry S Truman, became a haberdasher of men's hats, shoes, and furnishings. Unfortunately, credit sales bankrupted him. "Too much on the cuff," he would say in later years, "too little into the till." What could he do?

Chapter 7

Silent Movies

In Java, three thousand years ago, enterprising showmen devised the earliest method of projecting moving images. Bright light was passed through manipulated puppets made of animal skin and then projected onto a flat surface. These moving shadow-figures played out dramas to dialogue and music. From Java, these plays spread to India, then to Europe and were known in Paris as the Ombres Chinoise: Shadow Play.

In the fifteenth century, Leonardo da Vinci described a device using light from the sun reflected from a subject into a small hole containing a lens, thence into a darkened room, producing an image on a screen. This device, known as a camera obscura, embraces all of the principles of the projector: light source, subject, lens, and screen.

By the nineteenth century, itinerant magic lantern showmen were traveling from village to village in Europe, their limelight projectors strapped onto their backs. They would secure a hall, set up their equipment, and fire the lime. The clear white light produced would be focused onto images painted on a slide, then projected through two or more lenses onto a screen. The resulting visual images delighted audiences in numerous small towns and villages throughout Western Europe.

It was not until George Eastman introduced the Kodak camera in 1888 with its box, lensed peephole, and a roll of negative paper, that the raw material for the movies became available. Inventors rushed to use this new medium of permanently inscribing figures on cellulose. The wizard of Menlo Park, Thomas Alva Edison, devised the kinetograph camera using ideas from Etienne-Jules Marey. This French chronophotographer had devised a gun capable of recording several phases of movement upon a photographic surface. Edison took Marey's animation on cellulose idea, perforated the sides of film to make it move, and split the 70-millimeter film of Eastman in half, creating the present-day standard of 35 millimeters.

Inspired by Edison's kinetograph, the Lumiere brothers introduced the cinematograph. In December 1895, the first moving pictures were shown to a paying audience. Their motion picture camera and projector was based on the principle of the sewing machine, which drove a needle through fabric moved by the machine. The device held perforated film still during exposure to light, and then the mechanism of metal pins in the perforations moved the film quickly to the next exposure. These images, captured onto cellulose nitrate, were then projected as moving images onto a screen. But projection lighting was a problem; heated ether and lime were tried, but they caused fires. Finally, electrically fired carbon arcs were used. These proved to be a safer method of producing enough light for the projection of movies.

In the first decade of the 20th century, there was a need in Hawai'i for some form of wholesome entertainment. Republican and missionary morality could not countenance the mind-bending use of opium by the Chinese. After all, it was Queen Lili'uokalani's threat to legalize opium that was one of the reasons given by the revolutionists for the overthrow of the Hawaiian Kingdom. The Filipino plantation workers loved rooster fighting, but this was gambling and evil. With upwards of ten male laborers to every woman, the oldest profession in the world illicitly provided unwholesome entertainment.

The need for "good, clean" evening fun gave W.A. Fernandez the opportunity to become, as he would style himself, "the showman of the Pacific." One night, as he strolled through Honolulu, he saw a handbill advertising a brand new entertainment medium: silent movies. He bought a ticket and went to the show. It was a delightful evening; the flickering images projected on a white screen excited him to a greater degree than the Western Union word images of a championship fight. He could see the punches landing, watch the grimacing of the injured fighter and, in his mind, translate the screen action into his own words. Best of all, there were no charge accounts allowed at the box office. To see the flicks, a patron paid his nickel in advance. His previous business ventures had failed because of too much credit and a failure to pay.

Equally impressive to W.A. were the crowds at the theater who enjoyed watching the jerky, grainy, flickering, silent images. These crowds included all ethnic groups, many of them not knowing a word of English. It dawned on W.A. that people of all nations could understand pantomime and that silent gesturing images had a universal audience with no language barriers. He remembered the crowds at the Western Union office thirsting for the entertainment provided by the descriptive written word, words that could be translated into a mental visualization of a boxing event. Yet the word images provided by Western Union were in English and only the literate could understand and translate the meaning of English words into some form of visual action.

In contrast to word images, visual images in the silent movies projected onto a screen real life pictures of actors and lands far away. These actors mimicked, in silent photographs, love, anger, fear, courage, heroism and many other human emotions. Literacy in English was not necessary to understand these pantomimes. The "silents" were a unique means of conveying ideas to the broad spectrum of humanity. W.A. realized that here was a medium that he could sell to anyone, especially the multi-ethnic races that had come to Hawai'i to work in the sugar cane fields.

Seeking out the entrepreneur of the flicks, Fernandez made a deal with him; for a cash payment of $300, he became a part owner in this fledgling movie enterprise. His new partner promised to teach him the movie business and especially how to operate and service the equipment. W.A. believed that he had made a great bargain, but after six months the man absconded with all the money. This was not an irretrievable disaster. It was a blessing. The cash was gone, but "my partner left me with the movie equipment and knowledge of how to operate it," he laughed, recounting the event many years later.

Like the wandering lanternists of the previous century, Fernandez decided to become a pioneer Hawaiian showman. There were sugar plantation villages all over the Hawaiian Islands. Chinese, Japanese, Filipinos, Koreans, Portuguese, Spaniards, and other ethnic laborers populated them. They could understand the pathos and the triumphs portrayed by visual images. His Western Union and silent movie experiences in Honolulu convinced him that this new medium of communication could be universally understood and enjoyed. In plantation village after village, he showed his silent one-reelers. Chaplin, Jeffries, John Henry Johnson and Tom Mix, mimicked, boxed, or fought the Indians to the awe and delight of his multi-racial audiences.

In 1910, W.A. began traveling from island to island showing his movies. It was while astride his white horse, towing his movie camera and equipment on the trail between Kapa'a and Kilauea, that he had frightened his future wife.

Yet what the children remember of W.A. Fernandez was not a terrifying man in white, but the pictures that he would bring to their villages of a far away world. My aunts told me that in the evening they and other *keiki* (children) would be taken by *tutu* (grandmother) to a hall where they would lie against each other, waiting for the movie to start. When the lamps went out, an infernal racket erupted as Fernandez started up his car. Electricity, generated by the internal combustion engine, fired up the lighting for the projector. Once it was lit, W.A. shut down the noise and ran to his camera. Projection of the flicks might be onto a sheet, a screen, or even a wall. After an hour of silent movies, *tutu* would come for the *keiki*. Hand-in-hand, they would go home and talk about the show while eating snacks before going to bed.

Chapter 8

Pineapple

Before World War I, schooling was a limited experience on Kaua'i. Children received a basic education and, after elementary school, the young were expected to work. If additional education was needed, a family had to bear the expense of sending a child to Honolulu.

A good Catholic, Joseph Scharsch had twelve children and did not have the means to educate them. It became the responsibility of each of his children to earn money and help the eldest receive an education. On completing fifth grade, Agnes Scharsch went to work and provided money for her two older brothers to attend school in Honolulu.

Pineapple, discovered by Columbus on his second voyage to South America, was first grown commercially in Hawai'i in 1899. Initially, it was a struggling industry. Yet with James Dole's insight and ability, the Hawaiian Pineapple Company was organized in 1901. Soon it was providing three-quarters of the pineapple sold on the world's market.

The promise of good profits induced Hawaiian Canneries Co. to establish itself in Kapa'a in 1913. The cannery was located on Kuhio Highway at the southernmost edge of town, near the current Waia'kea Canal. Pay was minimal for cannery workers. Where Papa Scharsch might make a dollar a day as a field *luna* for Makee, fourteen year old Agnes earned four cents trimming and cutting pineapple.

Agnes Scharsch was a good worker. Her European father had taught her responsibility, honesty, and the giving of a full day's work for a day's wages. Soon her pay rose to five cents and then, with a promotion to floor supervisor, twenty-five cents. Agnes helped her family and yet saved enough money so that in later years she could say, "I built our home on pineapple savings and Bill and I moved in on the day we got married." It was the custom in olden times for families to pay cash for everything. Marriage could wait until you built, furnished your home, and paid for it.

The cannery changed Kapa'a. Once it started, the town came alive. Japanese who had completed their plantation work contracts moved in and opened mom and pop grocery stores. Portuguese opened dairy farms in the hinterland or repair shops in Kapa'a. Former plantation laborers became farmers, raising pineapple and other crops for sale. Service businesses started: the slop-gatherer who came to homes to take the garbage as feed for his pigs, the fish monger selling fish on the street, the cattle rancher who slaughtered cows and provided fresh meat to the market, the traveling wagon man hawking fresh fruits and vegetables.

The town became a kaleidoscope of names from every nation: Wong, Nakamura, Kubota, Rodrigues, Dikalato, Scharsch, Morgan, Thronas, Keahi, and others who made up the rainbow colors of Hawai'i. It became an integrated multi-racial town, containing an extraordinary mix of people living and working together in harmony.

By the time the First World War was over, the economy of Hawai'i was established: it was sugar cane, pineapple, and the military. Hawai'i was "Big Five" dominated, Republican, and conservative in its politics. Who were the "Big Five?" They were Caucasians who had created the economy of Hawai'i, helped overthrow the Hawaiian monarchy, and monopolized every aspect of its life. It was a paternalistic society with a clear division between the ruling class and the rest of the population.

Most Hawaiians were living by the sea, either as squatters or renters. Their habitats were grass shacks and their homes without amenities. Some, fortunate enough to work for the plantation, had slightly better living conditions, but there were very few who could buy land.

The missionaries had made sure that the natives covered their bodies, were given a language, and taught to sing hymns. Though poor, Hawaiians were caring people who followed native tradition by sharing everything they had with anyone. *"E komo mai"* is a phrase typifying Hawaiian style hospitality: "come in, my home is yours." It was not in their nature to fight the system but to get along with the other immigrants and accept their lot in life.

The inter-breeding between Hawaiians and immigrants from Asia and Europe had slowed the decimation of the Hawaiian race. Infant mortality was still high and disease took its toll of lives, but the part-Hawaiian had a higher survival rate than those of full blood. This inter-breeding had another effect on the native race; it interjected the desire to get ahead in life. It was not uncommon to say to a part-Hawaiian that his Chinese blood made him smart with money or his European blood made him smart at school. An Asiatic or Caucasian parent moved a Hawaiian child from the apathy of living in a tropical paradise to a new world of accomplishment.

Chapter 9

A Partnership

After the European peace makers at Versailles ensured a second world war by their humiliation of a defeated Germany, W.A. Fernandez also felt defeated by the inconstancy of his first wife. During World War I, he had come to Kaua'i to serve as a theater agent for Consolidated Amusement Company. He rented a hall from Joe Scharsch, opened a theater in Kapa'a, and installed his first wife as its manager while he performed his agent duties for Consolidated.

Show business in Kapa'a was profitable because of the pineapple cannery, but the first Mrs. Fernandez was unhappy. For a city girl, there was no society in the town, no excitement, only the boredom of work. Everything closed down at sunset. Rock fever is a common ailment for newcomers to Kaua'i and the 'bon vivant' is likely to catch it and leave the island to seek a cure. The first wife of W.A. left with the theater projectionist for Honolulu, taking the movie receipts with her.

Devastated by this betrayal, W.A. was rescued by Joseph Scharsch. When Fernandez advised him he had no money, Scharsch gave W.A. use of the theater rent free. When he said that he needed a ticket seller and collector, Joe answered, "how about my daughter Agnes?" With her help, Fernandez made a new beginning. It would lead to a new partnership. W.A. proposed marriage to his young employee.

"You should consider carefully what you are saying," advised Agnes. "Best that you take the time to be certain of your intentions before I say yes." She sensed that emotionally and psychologically, there was much for W.A. to resolve. "You have often spoken of taking your movies to the Orient. Why not take a vacation from Hawai'i for a time, and think things over? If you still want to marry, ask me again when you return."

Agreeing, W. A. packed up his cameras and booked ship's passage for Yokohama in 1921. For the next five years, he showed his movies in the Philippines, Thailand, Japan, and China. Pantomime, the art of the mime, has a transcending universal appeal for audiences of all nations. There is little difference between the art form of Marcel Marceau and the carbon-lighted and projected images from frames of film onto a silent screen. Fernandez, whether in Manila or Bangkok, delighted and excited these audiences with the pathos and comedy of human emotions created on film by movie studios located in far away California.

Significant changes occurred in Kapa'a while W.A. was away; a great fire in 1923 devastated most of the town. A fire break saved the properties of Scharsch and Morgan. For a time Kapa'a seemed threatened with extinction, but residents pulled together to rebuild.

The Hee Fat building across from the Roxy lot is symbolic of the architectural style of the reconstruction period of the town. Today, Kapa'a owes much of its character to the cleansing effect of that fire. Old shanties were eliminated. Better-sited streets and improved construction methods replaced the hastily thrown up structures of the early days of its growth.

On his return to Kapa'a, W.A. Fernandez again proposed marriage to Agnes. She accepted and the promises were fulfilled on September 17, 1927. The wedding party was held at their new home in Waipouli, built by Agnes's savings from her cannery days.

With his second marriage, W.A. settled in Kapa'a to stay. He leased an unused meeting hall in the Makee-created village of Kealia and another hall from C. Brewer & Company, owners of Kilauea Sugar Plantation. In a matter of a few short years, Fernandez became a movie magnate, operating a string of three theaters on Kaua'i, but, except for the home that Agnes built, he remained a landless Hawaiian.

Chapter 10

A Dot in the Pacific

"Hawai'i is a dot in the Pacific Ocean," I answered my teacher's question. This pronouncement startled the second grade class at Kapa'a Grammar School. Nervously clutching my tin soldier, I looked with embarrassment around the room. The answer reflected my impression of Kapa'a. Without a radio, we were isolated from the rest of the world by a vast ocean. In China, Japanese soldiers raped Nanking and Japanese aircraft bombed the American gunship Panay. Thousands of miles away in Europe, Hitler was plotting to attack Austria.

My family was on the mainland preparing for the building of the first and only theater that dad would ever own. I had been *hanai* to Aunt Catherine Morgan and lived in the center of Kapa'a.

As a child growing up in that cannery town in the 1930's, the ocean was mother, friend, and playground. Other than the movies and the occasional carnival, there was little else to do; the town continued its plantation lifestyle by rolling into bed every night at sunset. Yet the ocean was always there, providing great adventure above and below its surface, morning, noon and night. Polo may have been the sport of kings, but surfing was the sport of Hawai'i. Early Hawaiians hewed boat-shaped boards from forest logs that were hand-honed and rubbed until smooth to the touch. At Waikiki, Wailua, and Kapa'a, surfers rode on water as the surging ocean waves hurled them towards shore.

I had no money to buy a surfboard, yet a cast-away ironing board was a great substitute for a tree. A bar placed in front of the bare wood provided steering of a sort. This piece of surfing equipment had its drawbacks. Unless you kept its head above the wave at all times, the ironing board would dive for the bottom, hurling you onto sharp coral. The frothing surge would tumble your body along the reef as it rushed to the shore. Bruised, gasping for air, I would pull myself from the foam and charge out to sea to catch another wave.

Providing even more surfing excitement as well as the experience of cooperation and teamwork, was sailing a tin canoe. To build such a craft, a piece of discarded corrugated tin roofing had to be scrounged up. Bend, then nail, one end around a 2 x 4 block of wood, and you had a prow. Form and nail the other end around a half-moon-shaped wooden stern. Apply roof-tar to the cracks, holes, and wooden parts to make the ship water tight and *voila*, a canoe.

Without outriggers, the narrow tin canoe was as tippy as an Azorean whaling boat and, when hit broadside by a wave, it would turn over and sink. Paddling such a vessel took great effort and seamanship; push too hard in any direction and you were likely to turn, spill, and submerge. It took cooperation for two young boys, working as a team, to move the unstable craft through the sea and avoid sinking.

Learning to paddle a tin canoe taught the basics of societal living: working together and not against each other. Gently paddle on the right, then the left; keep the prow pointing into the waves; do not let it turn in the slightest. If it did, the craft would roll over and *auwe*, too bad, it filled with water and sank.

To play Cowboys and Indians, we would pull out tassels from budding cane stalks, trim the ends, shove a nail into one end, grab duck quills, trim, then tie them to the other end, *voila*, an arrow. The bow was the easy part; cut a suitable piece of hau wood and bend it with a string. The six-gun was a sling shot fashioned from the Y of an ironwood branch. Propellant power was supplied by a cut up inner tube with pine cones for ammunition.

I mention these things just to show that in Kapa'a, a kid had to make everything he played with. There was no variety store to buy from and we had no money anyway. Besides, supplies from off-island came infrequently to Kaua'i. As an example, mail service was a joke. It took six months to get my free Superman kit from New York.

Despite having nothing and making everything to play with, we had fun. We were kids of all races: Filipinos, Japanese, Chinese, Portuguese, and Hawaiians; there were even two Russian boys living in Waipouli, Archie and Ivan. They called themselves white Russians. I learned later that it wasn't the color of their skin, but their family's support of the Tsar, that made them white Russians as opposed to the Bolsheviks, who were red Russians.

These two Russians were crazy guys, very athletic and aggressive. They made swords, shields, and taught us about knighthood. Caped in cast-off table cloths and crowned with coconut helmets, we would batter each other with ironwood sticks and defend with shields of lauhala mats.

My Aunt Catherine was the "plantation clock." Every morning she got up at 4:30 and shut off the kerosene lantern in the hallway. In the kitchen, she rattled the stove as she prepared breakfast. No one in the household worked for the plantation anymore, but for many years Catherine's husband, Edward Morgan, did. Even though he was dead, she followed the routine of early rising to get people off to work before the sun rose. At night, the family knew when it was time for bed; it was the moment that Aunt Katie lit the kerosene lantern and put it in the hallway.

During the school year, I would get up with the "plantation clock," dress, creep into the kitchen for a quick breakfast, where you were seen and not heard, then off to school. Bare foot, in shorts and tee shirt, I kicked up dust with scores of other kids heading up the hill to Kapa'a School.

The teachers were part-Hawaiian, Portuguese, and Japanese. Three of them were family. Oh, that was not good. It was expected that I would do better than others. Maybe I was naughty, stupid, or just plain picked on because the discipline wreaked upon me was harsh: open your hand and be whacked with a ruler or whipped on the bare legs with a stick. In my youth, at and after school, my legs broke a few sticks.

All of us had the same look, the rice bowl haircut. Every two weeks you marched into Shinto's barber shop. It would be crowded with kids. He would plunk the rice bowl on your head and shave away what was beneath it, one style for all. Like the ditty, *shave and a haircut, two bits*, the shearing cost twenty five cents.

People were very hospitable in Kapa'a. I could play at anyone's house and eat with any race, except the ruling class *haole*. They lived in the exclusive areas far from Kapa'a.

I liked eating with the Chinese. They made delicious dishes out of scraps. I would always hang around a Chinese house when the father made char sui pork. You knew he was smoking the sugared pig, because the sweet smell wafted all over the neighborhood.

Hawaiians were especially fun to be with, maybe because I was half-Hawaiian and as my father would say, "black as the ace of spades." Anytime you went to a Hawaiian house, the call went out: "Come, eat." The food was great: poi, pig cooked in the ground or wrapped in leaves, raw fish, limpets, sea weed, and dried octopus. Oh, what a meal. It's a wonder that I remained skinny.

As I said earlier, the sea was important as a source of recreation, but it was also important as a place to learn co-operation and the joy of working with other people to achieve a common goal. I'm speaking of communal net fishing, a *hukilau*, meaning "pull in the net."

First, you must be patient. A fisherman might have to wait for days for a school of fish to enter a local bay and approach close enough to shore to be caught by surrounding nets. Once the fish came within a reasonable capture distance from the beach, the *hukilau* action would get under way. For a young boy, there was excitement, adventure, and an education when you participated in this great fish harvest.

I sometimes visited my cousins, the Akana family in Kalihiwai Bay, where John Akana, father of the clan, sat on his perch on a high hill overlooking the green-blue waters of the semi-circular bay. He would study the ocean looking for a large red clump of fish. When he saw darting dark shadows radiating out and clumping back into a large ball in the water, he would beg, "Give us a break. Come in, Come in." Yet the great school of *akule* (big-eyed scad) would feed just outside the bay, beyond reach.

Old John would cast about for lucky omens, even mutter prayers. But don't come up to his hill wearing red shorts. "Auwe" (too bad), he would say when he saw the red swim suit. "We are *make loa,* (dead) all *pau* now (finished). It is whitewash for today."

Days would drift by as the *akule* dawdled just beyond the reach of nets. In the ocean depths, they appeared like a huge red ink spot on a blue blotter. The mass of fish would tease John as the red clump drifted close to shore, then rolled back into deeper water.

Yet, on the dawning of the right day, *lanalana*, the spider, spun its web near John's lookout point. The dew, from the early morning cold, formed droplets of water that clung to the tendrils of the thin gossamer netting. Rays of the sun struck the spider's trap, flashing through the droplets, creating tiny rainbows, a good omen.

From the deep blue water, the great red ball of fish inched into the bay. The round shape of the clumped fish flashed into spikes as predators struck into the pile of *akule* scattering them. This piecemeal darting of the fish would jumble back into a spherical shape as their herd instincts clumped them together for safety. Like a whirling star, the deep red mass of *akule* swirled into Kalihiwai Bay as the sharks' feeding frenzy drove the hordes into shallow water.

John Akana jumped up, waving wide green ti leaves, signaling to men below. "*Hele mai*! Go! Go! Go!" he shouted, pointing his ti leaves toward the sea.

Grabbing their boats, the fishermen manhandled them into the ocean. Cresting waves tossed the crafts high into the air. As the vessels rolled into the troughs of passing waves, the men leaped in and Boy Akana took his command position in the stern of one of them. Old

John waved his ti leaves seaward, "Eh, dat way!" Boy pointed and oarsmen pulled against the sea, their crafts leaping over waves as they headed out. Playing out from the lead boat were two ropes attached to a net, each end held by men on shore.

Directed by John's semaphore leaves, the fishing boats sped into the bay, the lead vessel paying out net, the second moving outside its wake. Both crafts skimmed the water, hurled with barbaric force by straining oarsmen. To make the catch, speed is essential for man is the greatest predator of all, and fish can sense his presence. Once aware of the hunters with their webs of cord, the great mass of fish could scatter and be gone.

"*Auhe oe!*" (You, go there!) John screamed from his vantage point above the bay. Although he could not be heard, the turn message in his ti leaf signals was unmistakable. "Pull on da left!" yelled Boy. "Rest on da right!"

With skill, the straining men turned the lead boat lengthwise against the surge of the sea; the first part of the circle had begun. Pulled towards bottom by weights attached to the lead line, net sizzled into the water. At the opposite end, the float line, with its multiple egg-shaped corks attached to it like rosary beads, popped to the surface.

Once the first net was payed out, Boy shouted, "You da kine *pau*! Stop!" Pointing to the second boat he yelled, "Eh, you, come quick." With both boats pounding alongside each other, Boy sewed the end of the net in the first boat to an end of the net in the second boat.

Atop the hill, John screamed, "Go! Go!" Sea noise and wind drowned out his raving. Old John screamed again, fearful that the mass of *akule* would escape. But sewing nets together in wave-smashed boats is not an easy task.

Finally, Boy finished and urged his second crew, "*Huki! Huki!*" (Pull! Pull!) The second boat shot forward, Boy paying net into the sea.

John continued to scream. He waved his ti leaves like a windmill. With all his energy, he willed his men to move faster.

As the second net splayed into the water, Boy grunted, "too deep!" The corks of the float line struggled to rise to the surface. Would the fish escape over this gap? The fishermen would have to trust that the *akule* would stay close to the bottom of the bay.

After many minutes, John signaled his men to turn toward shore. Exhausted, they pulled toward the sand. Short of a wave-smashed beach, two boatmen leaped into the ocean and swam to eager hands waiting on the shore. Women grabbed ropes from the swimmers and pulled the net in. The fish were trapped.

John Akana descended from his lookout, ordering his son to gather more nets and surround the fish again and then once again. With the third set of nets in place, John felt that his catch was secure. Akana's plan was to keep the fish alive and confined as long as possible, emptying each set of nets as needed to meet the demand for fish.

Meanwhile, people from nearby towns and villages came to Kalihiwai to help in the *hukilau* They were joined by fish mongers in trucks and wagons eager to buy. The extraordinary size of this catch was soon evident; all of Hawai'i would be well fed. Bamboo baskets were brought out, dipped into the mass, hauled out, and taken to waiting vendors.

Flashing in the water among the hordes were fins. Caught in the press of fish, predators were grasped by the tail, manhandled from the squirming mass and dumped onto the beach, to be seized by Chinese eager to make shark fin soup. By the second day, big sharks had torn large rents in the first net as they desperately attempted to escape. Swimming in the water between the second and third net, you came upon them, their bellies satiated with fish. They wallowed in the sea like helium filled balloons. A diver could push them away as he worked on rents.

When the third net was emptied, John divided fish among the many races that had come to help. There was no discrimination; all shared equally. This is the Hawaiian way.

Once the division was completed, the party began. Fish were grilled in fireplaces scooped from the sand. Chicken and vegetables slowly stewed in a great black pot nestled in a fireplace on the shore. Rice, poi, fruits, haupia, kulolo, cakes and goodies filled picnic tables and beach mats as people gathered to celebrate the great catch. Children splashed in the waves, chased each other and pretended to push away sharks as the men sat in the shade, making quiet, satisfied conversation while they repaired torn nets. Women in their colorful clothes laughed as they prepared food and organized dinner.

As the feasting began, someone strummed a guitar. Soon, a couple of ukuleles and the twang of a bass tub joined in. Beer flowed. Everyone sang Hawaiian songs. A grandmother started a slow hula soon to be joined by another, then another. After a hard day's work, it was hang loose time. Before the beach fire, little tots fell asleep as the adults partied into the night.

This was the happy life in Kapa'a before the war. It was school for part of the day, then swimming, surfing, octopus fishing, netting, torch-light fishing, and an occasional communal event, like the *hukilau*. Other than separation from the ruling class, there was no discrimination despite the multiple races living in the town. Tolerance was universal and stress was non-existent. It was peaceful, for there were no products to buy and greed to acquire was absent. If you needed food or clothes or services, you traded for it and the value of what you gave could be big or small. No matter. Without money, you had no worries, for you made what you needed, and desired less. Events occurring far away were heard only as scratchy sounds on my cousin's crystal set.

Chapter 11

The Fernandez Legacy: The Roxy

I have said that Kapa'a was unique and I have described for you the tolerance of others that existed in the town. But it had another characteristic: it was not dominated by a plantation. It had workers who were employed by Makee but they were field *luna* like Scharsch and Morgan. To the north were the sugar mills at Kealia and Kilauea, to the south, more mills, but none in Kapa'a.

Why did Kalakaua open a mill there? Because it was land he controlled and that his *hui* (club) could use for a pittance. Though his venture failed, it had a salutary effect; the town was built on what became government land, was subdivided into lots, and acquired by citizens at an affordable price. This meant that former plantation laborers could become entrepreneurs, open shops, and develop a middle class existence.

Contrast this with a plantation town where all the land was owned by the plantation and workers lived a feudal existence in segregated camps. Free enterprise was not possible. The company controlled the lives of their workers and these men were required to buy what they needed from the company store. Invariably, they owed more than they earned. There was no time for fun; just work from dawn to dusk at a pittance wage.

Living conditions in the labor camps in 1930 were abysmal. There were twenty five to thirty five homes in a camp. There were separate camps for each race. Most homes were four rooms with two families to a house. If it was a Filipino camp, there might be six to eight men living in the same residence. Furniture was sparse; a mat on the floor was a bed, windows were screen-less, netting providing the only protection from mosquitoes. Kerosene lamps or candles furnished light. If a family was lucky, they had a wood burning, smoky, iron stove; otherwise cooking was done on a wood fire outside. A local stream or a community tub were the bathing facilities; the same stream used for bathing sometimes served as a toilet, otherwise smelly, unsanitary outhouses were available.

Wages were meager. To survive, families raised pigs, cattle, chickens, and ducks, plus grew their own vegetables in small gardens. Bartering and trading were common. The killing of rats supplemented income.

Plantation towns were noisy and dirty. Grinding sugar cane into molasses went on all day and into the night. Smoke from the crushing and cooking filled the air with soot. Tons of trash littered the dirt pathways and iron red soil colored everything.

This was not true in Kapa'a. My home town, in the 1930's, was a trash-free community. It had the most popular non-exclusive beach on Kaua'i, a broad crescent of white sand stretching for half a mile from the present day Moikeha canal to the Waia'kea canal. Scores of coconut trees shaded the shore. Stretching south from Kapa'a Park, there were three rows of magnificent ironwoods that protected the shoreline and acted as a windbreak. A train track curved along the beach, servicing the pineapple cannery and the sugar mill in Kealia. Raw sugar and canned pineapple were hauled by the train to Ahukini for shipment overseas. When Lihu'e Plantation acquired Makee in 1934, trains hauled cut cane stalks from the Kapa'a area to the Lihu'e mill for grinding.

Hawaiian Pineapple Cannery was near Waia'kea. Bordering this sluggish waterway was American Can Company. In total, the two business complexes were the biggest buildings in town.

In my time, Waia'kea was not a running stream; for most of the year it was bottled up by sand dunes and dead coral flung ashore by ocean waves. The result was a pestilent swamp called by my mother, *wailana*, still water. Its sides were steep and the unmoving water dark and mysterious. To keep children away from this dangerous place, we were told it was the home of the dead, and ghosts would eat you if you fell in. In the depths of the listless murk you could see a rectangular box, shaped like a coffin. There were whispers in the neighborhood that this was the home of Dracula, and in the night he would come from his grave searching for blood.

But this boogie man talk never kept a curious kid away from anything. My friends and I would play by the dead pool, throwing rocks into it hoping to wake up the vampire. One day, as I was peering into the dim waters searching for the Transylvanian Count, I fell in. Screaming my head off, I felt Dracula's icy grip on my bare legs. I scraped the steep sides of the pond with my finger nails seeking to escape. My head dipped into the murky water and I thought the end had come. Then my foot touched a rock. I found another and climbed out. I didn't die from ghosts, but I did get violently sick.

South of this bog stretched sand dunes that continued until one came to the suburb of Waipouli. Sometime in the early part of the twentieth century, a developer replaced sand with bungalows. He planted rows of ironwood trees along the shore and exotic plants and flowers. I mention this area since it became home for the middle class families of Kapa'a, including my parents.

Set back fifty feet from the crescent beach of the town were wooden houses where poor Hawaiians, Chinese, Filipinos, and Koreans lived. Next was a line of commercial buildings fronting Kuhio Highway. On the *ma kai* (ocean) side of the roadway, facing the site of the future Roxy Theater, were the Hee Fat building and Chinese shops. On the *ma uka* (mountain) side of the highway, stretching from Kukui Street north on Kuhio Highway, were a string of Japanese stores running all the way to Moikeha stream. North of the stream was the U.S. Post Office, the courthouse, a repair shop, retail stores, the electric company, and homes of former Portuguese plantation workers.

Kukui Street wound from its intersection with Kuhio Highway around the town, heading westward into the hills. Where Kukui Street climbed into the hinterland was a rice field and, adjacent to it, a large Filipino labor camp called Pueo. It was a lively place to visit on holidays, with its cock fights, boxing matches, and other activities. Occasionally, the police decided to make a raid and then you would see a sudden disappearance of roosters, gambling paraphernalia, and women. I could say more about vice in Kapa'a, but that is not the purpose of this story. Beyond Pueo camp was a large open air garbage dump and a Chinese cemetery. Further into the hill country were farms, where immigrants raised pigs, cattle, and produce.

Paralleling Kukui Street is a short roadway called Lehua. Along the roadway, the Makee plantation built a spur rail line heading into the hill area beneath Sleeping Giant Mountain. On the *ma kai* side of the tracks lived the Morgan and Scharsch families, along with Chinese who had developed the local rice fields and then became business proprietors in Kapa'a. On the other side were more Chinese families.

Beyond these Chinese homes were rice fields and swamps, the latter very dangerous to walk in. When heavy rains came, up to twenty five inches in a day, this marsh land would flood. The still waters of Moikeha and Waia'kea would overflow and the town would be submerged. Though this flooding caused great damage, it was fun for kids as a large variety of fish and crawly things were caught in your front yard, plus you could paddle your tin canoe along the roadways of the town.

It took World War II to convince the government that something needed to be done. Moikeha and Waia'kea canals were constructed and with this new drainage system *wailana* and its ghosts disappeared and the marshland shrank. Today, Kapa'a is no longer underwater during rainy periods and the area beyond Lehua Street has been developed into public parks.

In the center of town is the First Hawaiian Church. It has a long history dating back more than a hundred years. In its graveyard, my great grandmother is buried as well as other relatives. I have wonderful memories of the church: the singing of hymns and the services in Hawaiian, the luaus that would be held there, and as a place where my father first ran his movies in the town.

I used the phrase "non-exclusive beach," to describe the Kapa'a ocean front as a place where the local people came and enjoyed the sea. In the 1930's there was a clear divide between the families of the plantation owners and the rest of the common folk. There were beaches and enclaves where entry by natives and immigrants was prohibited. In this hierarchy of class, the descendants of the missionaries and those of New England stock were at the top. They owned most of the island, controlling access to select parts of the sea. In fairness, I should point out that, despite this class separation, the wealthy Caucasians exhibited a paternalistic philanthropy, providing land for schools, establishing Wilcox and Mahelona hospitals, fostering parks like Lydgate in Wailua, museums, and libraries.

Next in line to the upper class Caucasian, came Europeans like Scharsch and Morgan who had saved their plantation earnings, built homes, and raised families. At the bottom rung of the social scale were the Hawaiians and former contract laborers who came to the town to start a new life. Because of its lower class roots, Kapa'a was not pretentious. It was a place of opportunity where a "have not" with integrity and skill could achieve prominence and be rewarded for ability.

Although my father was successful with the small theater that he leased, the Rialto, he dreamed of owning his own movie house. Encouraged by my mother, W.A. traveled to California, Washington D.C. and New York City, accompanied by Joe and Helen Rodrigues. His prime purpose was to visit U.S. movie theaters and arrive at a design for his future auditorium. When the group returned to Kaua'i, they related an unusual tale. Within two days of arriving in the nation's capitol, headlines in the Eastern press proclaimed that the country's most notorious bank robber, accompanied by one of his gunmen and a mysteriously beautiful woman, were sighted in a Washington D.C. restaurant. The news article included a picture of John Dillinger. With his moustache and dark hair, Joe Rodrigues was a dead ringer for Public Enemy Number One.

Touring and sightseeing ended, as the visitors from Hawai'i hid in their hotel. When Elliot Ness and his agents gunned down John Dillinger in Chicago, W.A., Helen, and Joe sighed in relief as their fears of an imminent mistaken-identity shooting ended. Yet even today there are news articles like the following: "The 1934 shooting is wrapped in mystery, starting with the elusive "Lady in Red," Anna Surge, who lured Dillinger to the Biograph Theater where he was slain, to claims that it wasn't really Dillinger who died that night on a Chicago sidewalk." (Palo Alto Daily News, Monday, February 23, 1998.) Is it possible that John Dillinger escaped the G-Men?

Traveling resumed with the news of Dillinger's demise. In New York, Fernandez fell in love with the 6,000 seat Roxy Theater. He determined to build his Kaua'i auditorium in the same grand style. On his return from his first trip to the big island of America, W.A. convinced Agnes that they should build a theater of their own in Kapa'a.

In those days, purchasing land by a Hawaiian was not an easy matter. From 1901, when the first Territorial Legislature convened, until 1954, Hawai'i was dominated by the Big Five companies. These were Castle and Cooke, Alexander & Baldwin, American Factors, Theodore H. Davies and Company, and C. Brewer and Company. The Big Five controlled more than half of the total land area of Hawai'i and 90% of its economy. The Federal Government and a handful of private trusts held forty-five percent of the remaining land. A meager five percent was owned by the multi-racial people who had come to work in the sugar fields and the native Hawaiian.

In the center of Kapa'a town was an acre of land owned by American Factors, the controlling shareholder of Lihue Sugar Plantation. W.A. decided to buy the acre. To acquire Big Five land, money was not enough. Plantation paternalism required that land sold must be used for a healthy moral purpose. To buy, W.A. needed to secure the approval of the *haole* father of Kaua'i by explaining his intentions. A movie theater that projected "wholesome family entertainment" was an approved purpose.

Five years before the "Day of Infamy," on the payment of $10,000, W.A. Fernandez acquired an acre bounded by Kuhio Highway, Kukui, Kauwila, and Ulu Streets in Kapa'a town. After the purchase, my family left for the mainland to plan and equip the theater, leaving me in the care of my aunt Catherine.

To design his dream, W.A. hired C. W. Dickey, the foremost architect in Hawai'i. On February 19, 1939, Dickey presented his plan for the largest and grandest theater in all of Hawai'i. When built, the Roxy would consist of a ground floor and a second floor balcony with an auditorium of 8,606 square feet and sufficient space for 1,050 seats. Roxy's interior would be decorated in the art nouveau style, with colorful carpets lining the hallways and a large second floor lounge and adjacent wash rooms. There were red seats with wood trim on the ground floor and top balcony, and plush blue metal chairs in the lower balcony.

The stage would be capable of holding a full orchestra and dancers. At the back of the stage would be the largest movie screen in Hawai'i. To the sides were dressing rooms for entertainers. The entire ensemble was hidden by rich, heavy, red velvet curtains. When they were opened, the huge silver screen and stage were overwhelming. The sound system was state of the art and the acoustics awesome, all designed by my cousin, Albert Morgan.

An outstanding, unseen feature was the projection room. In the early days of the movies, tragic fires erupted in theaters due to the use of two highly flammable chemicals; ether, as a source of light for projection and the highly combustible, cellular-nitrate-based, film used as an image-producing medium. A terrible fire occurred in 1897 at The Charity Bazaar in Paris, killing or severely burning more than 150 people. Since that tragic event, fear of fire in theaters became a prime concern. Roxy's projection room was encased in metal and then fireproofed with concrete. Specially designed and built, it would restrict a nitrate film fire to the projection room where it would burn itself out and not escape into the body of the theater. Because of its unique construction, the room was first built on the ground, and then installed by crane onto the upper floor of the theater.

At the front of the building, adjacent to the auditorium, Dickey designed two ground floor retail spaces. Above these were six rooms suitable for offices. The entire project cost $50,000. When completed, its three stories made it the tallest building in Kapa'a.

While the German military machine completed its occupation of Poland, and Stalin threatened to attack Finland, the Roxy Theater opened its doors. With this gala event, W.A. Fernandez no longer rented, no longer traveled from town to town showing his movies. Due to the unique character of Kapa'a, a landless Hawaiian had become an established business man in the Kaua'i community.

The Charles Kaneyama Orchestra created an atmosphere of charged excitement as Mr. and Mrs. Fernandez greeted friends, family, and well-wishers at the open doors of the Roxy Theater Saturday, November 18, 1939. It was a fun filled night of balloons, food, and music and the movie, *Lady of the Tropics*. One bizarre event marred a great evening. Agnes Fernandez owned one of the few yellow Ford coupes on the island with a rumble seat. In all of the excitement, Agnes decided to place her sleeping son in the rumble seat of a Ford parked in the theater lot. After the crowd left, she discovered that I was not in her car. Telephone calls to police and inquiries to locals were made. A yellow Ford coupe was traced to Kilauea and a frantic post-midnight ride ensued. I was found snoring in the back of a car. Why all the fuss? The long trip to Kilauea under the stars, the gentle rocking of the auto, produced one of the finest sleeps I have ever had.

The Roxy's bill of fare was a new movie every night. Tuesday featured a show from the Philippines. Wednesday heralded a drama. Thursday, a Japanese feature, either a love story or a samurai flick. Friday, a general audience movie or comedy would be shown. Saturday, at the matinee would be a serial and a good Hollywood drama. Sunday, would be a first rate movie. Monday, a double bill: a detective story and a cowboy show.

But more than movies played at the Roxy. Renowned artists from the mainland came to perform. These included opera arias and black spirituals sung by Marion Anderson, the classical violin of Yehudi Menuhin, and the Wagnerian voice of Lauritz Melchior. Stage shows from Japan thrilled mixed audiences. With its grand stage, the Roxy handled scores of actors and musicians with ease, and its acoustics produced memorable evenings.

At least twice a month on Saturday, it was lucky night. A huge wheel with multiple numbers was rolled onstage. A little music and away would spin the arrow. When it stopped on a number, the winner got a substantial prize, like a basket of groceries, or a cash reward.

Advertising for the Roxy was fun. There were the usual trailers shown each time a movie was performed. But the real sales pitch was passing out handbills. Off to Filipino camp with a drum and, like Pagliacci, "Boom, boom, boom," it would beat and I, a nine year old, would cry out, "The Roxy is featuring tomorrow night, Jose Castro and

Rene Lopez in a torrid drama of love, mystery, and death." Then I passed out handbills describing the feature in the language appropriate to the movie being shown.

Roxy's auditorium was divided into sections with a uniformed usher serving as a guide. Pricing varied from 20 cents up front; side seats, 40 cents; back rows and ground floor, 55 cents; balcony front rows, 55 cents; second level balcony, 40 cents. Second level balcony, at the very top, was always filled with lovers. Many romances and families started at the part of the Roxy auditorium closest to heaven.

For the first seven years of its show life, food was not served in the theater. Instead, you ate at the Roxy Sweet Shop or Stumpy's, an open air restaurant on the theater lot facing Kuhio Highway. The Sweet Shop offered great candies and ice cream sodas; hamburgers at Stumpy's were *'ono*, delicious. With Stumpy's and the theater crowd, Roxy square was a rocking, fun-filled place for locals to hang loose.

To show what an important role the theater played in the town, let me describe a night when Filipino movies were shown. After *pau hana* (end of work), Philippine Island men would wash, put on white shirts and ties, some would wear coats, and they would come to the movies an hour before show time. Patiently, they would wait for the doors to open, gossiping, telling stories, and so on. Once the ticket taker came, they filed into the auditorium chattering in their various dialects. When the lights went out, conversation ceased until the movie ended. After the show, they left peacefully for their labor camps.

The Roxy brought new life to the town. People who lived in Kapa'a remember the sounds from the movies filling the streets with music and laughter. No longer did the town live by the plantation clock and sleep when the sun went down. It remained lively well into the night. The theater with its huge silver screen, outstanding sound system, and state of the art movie projection brought magic to the lives of all of us. I can still remember *The Wizard of Oz* with its bigger-than-life actors, Technicolor scenes, and Judy Garland singing *"Over the Rainbow."* It was so overwhelming, that after the show I climbed the highest tree I could find and sang *"Over the Rainbow,"* believing that the wizard would come in his balloon and whisk me off to the Emerald City.

Prior to the Roxy, W.A. Fernandez had never had the luxury of theater ownership. Moving from town-to-town and renting halls or tents had meant that he always found a new and eager crowd ready to see the movies. Expenses were minimal and he supplied most of the labor. But once in a fixed spot with a 1,050 seat movie theater, his costs soared. The United States was in a recession. By 1940, W.A. began to feel an economic pinch. Soon, this Hawaiian entrepreneur was struggling to pay his bills.

Far, far away, another greater struggle was occurring. After crushing France by lightning war, the Nazis struck at England with mighty air fleets. In the Far East, Japan, emboldened by the success of the Germans, embarked on an ambitious plan: the creation of *The Greater East Asia Co-Prosperity Sphere*. Like a gigantic spider in the center of a web, Japan would sit in the center of its rising sun, and control all of the vast resources of Asia and dominate its people.

The movies were first used as a propaganda tool by Nikolai Lenin. After the Bolshevik revolution in 1917, he commissioned a "Red Train," and converted several railroad cars into movie theaters. The train steamed out of Moscow and into the countryside showing propaganda film to the Russian people to convince them that Communism was better than rule by a Tsar.

The Nazis adopted Lenin's scheme and developed their own propaganda films. Leni Riefenstahl's, "*Triumph of the Will*," filmed in 1934, depicted Hitler as a god descending from the sky, sent to bring back the glory days of the Aryan people. It convinced millions of Germans to follow the Nazi leader into the hell of war.

With Allied defeats in Europe and Asia, movies changed. It appeared as if President Roosevelt and Hollywood were using film to propagandize the American people to prepare for war. Movies no longer concentrated on love stories like *Shangri-La* starring Ronald Coleman or swashbucklers like *Robin Hood* or *Captain Blood*. In the year France fell, short subjects like the *March of Time* depicted the conflicts occurring in the world and the evils of Fascism and Imperialism. Memorable for me, was the story of the "*Fighting Irish*," an army regiment of New York's Rainbow Division. This unit was given its nickname by General Robert E. Lee at the Battle of Malvern Hill. They were so courageous that Stonewall Jackson said, "Here come those d--- Irish again."

The movie, *The Fighting '69th*, depicted the bravery of that Irish-American regiment from Brooklyn during World War I. It starred Pat O'Brien, playing Father Francis Duffy, and James Cagney. Especially heroic was Cagney who covered a live German grenade with his body to save his friends. He received a Best Actor Oscar for the movie, *Yankee Doodle*, yet in my mind, his greatest role was as the cocky, obnoxious, cowardly, heroic Irish soldier in *The Fighting 69*[th]. I re-named my tin soldier Sandy in his honor.

Yet despite this movie propaganda, war seemed far away. In 1941, Kaua'i was suffering a severe economic downturn and patrons were sparse at the Roxy. As Hitler launched his attack on Russia, code named Barbarossa, W.A. allowed his mortgage payments to lapse as he struggled to meet his other obligations. Soon, Bank of Hawai'i threatened foreclosure. By the first of December, he was six months in arrears and in danger of losing his dream. Like an albatross about his neck, his 1,050 seat Roxy was a folly. His foolishness for building such a large theater on Kaua'i, with its high operating cost and negligible attendance, was forcing him into bankruptcy. Venture after venture that he had tried over the past 45 years had been failures. Now, in early December of 1941, W.A Fernandez said, "Agnes, I am going broke again. I don't know what we are going to do."

Roxy Theater in New York City at 50th and 7th, home of the Roxyettes, precision dancers. Built in 1927 and named after noted theater operator Samuel "Roxy" Rothafel, it was billed as "the largest theater in the world." It had 6,000 seats and was demolished in 1960.

Architectural drawing of the Roxy by C.W. Dickey, the most prominent architect in Hawaii during the first half of the 20th century. After 29 years of traveling from plantation town to plantation town showing movies, W.A. Fernandez completed his dream, the largest showplace in Hawaii.

Roxy Theater was built and equipped in six months at a cost of $50,000, with a seating capacity of 1,050 seats. Two stores were in front of the building: Roxy Sweet Shop and Bata Shoe Store; the second floor had six offices. The Roxy had several firsts in Hawaii: fluorescent lighting, a parabolic floor (curved like a bowl) so all customers had a clear view, 15 foot breaks in the walls to improve acoustics; with 25 miles of wire, electricity could be controlled from the stage to the projection room.

Fans lined up for the afternoon show before the devastating flood.

Kapa'a flood, 1940. 25 inches of rain fell in 24 hours and the swamps overflowed. The town became a giant lake. Alice Morgan Paik at the prow, future husband Jack Paik at the oars, theater projectionist Harold Wong at the bow, with unknown fisherman, preparing to enter the theater.

Roxy Theater rises above the flood waters 3 feet deep.

Marion Anderson fought prejudice most of her life. Refused admission to the Philadelphia Music Academy, she received private singing lessons. Once her fame was established, she sought an engagement at Constitution Hall in Washington D.C. The Daughters of the American Revolution (DAR) refused to let her perform. Eleanor Roosevelt arranged to have her sing at the Lincoln Memorial in 1939, the same place that Martin Luther King gave his "I Have a Dream Speech," 27 years later. 75,000 people watched her sing.

The lawn at All Saints Church, Waipouli, Kaua'i, where I first met the Fighting 69th, in April of 1942. This is where I learned that war could be profitable.

Top: Stanley and Andy, soldiers of the 69th Regiment. Bottom: local boys who were in the Hawaii National Guard. Second from left is Uncle Jack Paik.

Scene from *Pagan Love Song*, 1950, shot at Horner Mansion, Wailua Bay. Foreground, Howard Keel and Esther Williams. Background, serving Mai Tais, Uncle Jack Paik.

Roxy Theater in 1969.

Iniki hit Kaua'i September 11, 1992. Pictures of the Roxy taken a week later.

Roxy front after Iniki.

Roxy being crushed November 2, 1992.

Chapter 12

The Day of Infamy

"Climb Mount Niitaka," ordered Admiral Yamamoto. The *Akagi*, *Kaga*, *Soryu*, *Hiryu*, *Zuikaku*, and *Shokaku* turned to the south. It was the mightiest fleet of aircraft carriers ever assembled and it was to undertake history's greatest naval air raid. Only once before had carrier aircraft attempted a wartime attack on ships. It happened on November 11, 1940, at the Italian naval base at Taranto, located in the great curve of the boot of Italy. British Fairey Swordfish launched from the decks of the *Illustrious* and *Eagle* torpedoed and sank battle wagons of the Italian navy in harbor. Inspired by this success, the Japanese Commander-in-Chief of the Combined Fleet, Admiral Isoroku Yamamoto conceived the plan of attacking the American Navy at Pearl Harbor. This foolish notion, of aircraft sinking battleships, had earlier secured for American General Billy Mitchell a court martial. Yet Yamamoto's plan had already been successfully executed at Pearl Harbor. American Admiral Harry F. Yarnell, as part of a military exercise, raided Pearl in the early morning of a Sunday in 1932.

Warning buzzers in six carriers sounded alarms near dawn on December 7, 1941. From his command ship, the *Akagi*, Vice Admiral Nagumo announced to his men, "As a symbol of victory, the flag flown by Admiral Togo at the battle of Tsushima Straits is being unfurled." Inspired by this announcement, three hundred and fifty men of the Imperial Japanese Air Force shouted defiant "*banzais*," leaped into their Mitsubishis and Nakajimas, and roared off the carrier flight decks into the rising sun.

Flying south over the gentle Pacific, the flight leader of the first wave of 207 bombers, fighters, and torpedo planes reported: "Pearl Harbor is asleep in the morning mist. It is calm and serene inside the harbor. Not even a trace of smoke is rising from the ships at O'ahu. The orderly groups of barracks, the wiggling white line of automobiles climbing up the mountain tops, the ships at anchor, are all fine objectives to attack." It was 7:55 A.M., December 7, 1941.

That day dawned as the most beautiful of Hawaiian days. A predicted storm did not strike the islands. With church bells peeling their joy, my family drove homeward from early morning mass. I watched the sun rise magnificently above the grip of the horizon, its golden rays reaching out to warm me. The gentle green-blue ocean glistened, reflecting the soft pinks and blues of the sun. Waves rolled lazily towards a sandy shore studded by palm trees curved stiffly at attention, their leaves barely rippling.

Our family had purchased a radio, a cone shaped brown box, and on arriving home, at 8:15 A.M., my father turned on the magic instrument to catch the early morning news. "This is no drill," blared the hysterical announcer. "We are under attack by Japanese aircraft! Pearl Harbor is in flames! Honolulu is being bombed! Remain indoors! We are signing off the air!"

Excited, I ran outside to see the air battle occurring one hundred miles away. My mother went crazy, screaming at me that I would be killed by flying bombs. Frightened, I returned indoors to hide, shivering in fear, under my bed. All that day and night, we expected an invasion at any moment. It was in this way that the "Day of Infamy" began. Sleepy, lazy, isolated, Hawai'i was no longer just a dot in the Pacific Ocean; it had become the center of a mighty struggle for control of the Pacific. By this act of war, our islands were forever changed.

Chapter 13

The War Years

With its attack on Pearl Harbor, the Empire of Japan believed it had secured a great military advantage. Eight of America's battlewagons were damaged or at the bottom of Pearl Harbor. More than a dozen other ships had been hit. The great naval base had been hurt so severely that Admiral Nagumo and his six aircraft carriers left Hawai'i with the belief that the U.S. Pacific fleet had been paralyzed for years to come.

Japan was free to pursue its imperial ambitions, protected by its navy and its ring of island fortresses in the Marshall, Gilbert, and the Mariana Islands. Within this ring, Japan intended to take the rich resources of Southeast Asia; conquer the Philippines, invade Australia, Samoa, and Hawai'i. Then, as Admiral Yamamoto boasted, "I will dictate the peace in Washington D.C."

A week after the attack, a furious storm struck Hawai'i, and it rained into Christmas. The only bright spot to relieve the bleakness of the blacked out nights and Kaua'i's helplessness was the heroics of Ben Kanahele.

A Japanese aircraft made a forced landing on the small, privately owned island of Ni'ihau. After the pilot's arrival, there was a confrontation between him and Ben Kanahele, the Robinson's headman on the "Forbidden Island." The pilot shot Ben three times. After the third shot, Ben got plenty *hu hu,* mad, grasped the man like a sheep, and hurled him against a rock wall. This would be the only American victory over the Japanese for the next several months.

The attack on Pearl Harbor was a catastrophe for Japanese-Americans living in Hawai'i. The military looked upon these citizens with suspicion. It was wrongly believed that they had signaled Nippon bombers and directed them to Pearl Harbor. Sabotage was suspected in the destruction of aircraft at Hickam Field in Honolulu. These suspicions were ill founded, but mutters of reprisals against the Japanese were not uncommon, and a few isolated incidents occurred after the air strikes.

In 1941, nearly forty percent of the population of the Hawaiian Islands was Japanese. It would have been an economic disaster to intern all of them in the U.S. In the aftermath of the attack, only a few from Hawai'i were sent to the relocation camps on the mainland. The vast majority of Hawai'i's Americans of Japanese ancestry (AJA) remained in Hawai'i, and thousands of young Nisei volunteered to serve in the United States Army. Exploits of these brave soldiers have been well chronicled; suffice it to say that they acquitted themselves with honor, great distinction and, with their blood, gave their all for the United States of America.

The Fernandez family learned there were unexpected advantages to war. Martial law was declared and a moratorium on all debts and obligations. W.A. was freed from the imminent foreclosure of his 1,050 seat folly. But would his gamble in building a large theater pay off or would he face a disaster if Kaua'i was invaded?

Before the year was out, Japan attacked Hawai'i again. A submarine surfaced outside of Nawiliwili Harbor on December 30, 1941. After firing a few rounds causing little damage, it submerged and left. This event underscored the weakness of Kaua'i; the sub's five-inch gun was more powerful than any cannon on the island. As long as enemy submersibles could inflict deadly damage with impunity, ships could not visit the Garden Island.

December and January were bleak during the day with homes and businesses blacked out at night. Japan was piling up victories in South East Asia and off the coast of Kuala Lumpur. With the invasion of the Philippines, some Filipino men armed themselves, openly patrolling the streets of Kapa'a looking for subversive activity.

February and March were worse; a Japanese submarine torpedoed the U.S. transport, Royal T. Frank, and a Japanese aircraft bombed Honolulu. Singapore, Borneo, Java, and Indonesia were occupied by Japanese troops. American forces in the Philippines had surrendered the main islands and retreated to Corregidor in Manila Bay. Wake Island and Guam were gone. There seemed to be nothing that could stop the Japanese juggernaut from owning the Pacific.

April found Kaua'i in a cold spell. Fears of invasion were prevalent, and plans were underway for guerilla warfare in the mountains should the Japanese invade. I was prepared for an attack. Every night I slept with my blue and red BB gun, filled with copper balls. In the daytime, I walked the streets with it over my shoulder ready to fight invaders. It sounds silly, but when you are isolated and fearful, you turn to any comfort you can find. I assure you that there were other boys who carried their BB guns with them.

One chilly morning at Easter time, I woke early and jumped from bed, eager for adventure. No one was allowed at the seashore a block from my house, so I headed inland toward All Saints Gym. My mother told me to leave the air rifle at home so I walked to the church grounds defenseless.

"Wow!" There were more Caucasian men there than I had ever seen in my entire life, and they looked like Sandy, my tin soldier, with reddish cheeks and light brown hair. "Wow!" I yelled a second time, these were boys from Brooklyn. "We are the Fighting Irish, the 69th Regiment from New York, come to save you from the Japanese," a soldier said. Then he whispered, "By the way, kid, do you know any young girls?" This would be an oft-repeated question in the days ahead.

A whole division of American soldiers, the Rainbow Division, had descended on Kaua'i. Their first duty was to protect the island from invasion, their second duty, to train for war in the Pacific. They performed their first duty with vigor. Barbed wire was strung along all of the beaches of the island. Machine gun pits and reinforced concrete bunkers were built at tactically significant seaside areas; one was on the shore near our home. Training for rigorous jungle warfare and amphibious landings was conducted. Men worked hard at developing the skills of warfare in a new venue of modern war, the Pacific and its many islands and atolls. Martial law was strictly enforced on Kaua'i. There was open hostility between these fighting men from the mainland and the Japanese-American citizens of Kapa'a, but no incidents occurred, however there was an attitude of, "shoot first and ask questions later."

Naïve, I didn't know any eligible girls to provide to the G.I. who asked me questions about available women, but I soon learned that Irish soldiers love to eat. They wanted cokes, donuts, hot dogs, candy, and ice cream. "Hey kid," soldiers would call out. "Get me some cokes."

Off into town on my bare brown feet I would run with the money given by Stanley, Andy, or Figueroa to buy goodies. Returning, I would pass out orders, get a tip, and off again to Kapa'a, making several round trips until the platoon sergeant said, "Scram kid." By that time money was jingling in my shorts. Like Mother Courage, I had found out that war was profitable. There was one disappointment; Pat O'Brien and James Cagney were not with the 69th regiment.

As an interesting aside, Joe Figueroa said that he was Italian and not Irish, but he was Catholic just like the other men. On Kaua'i, we were aware that Japanese on the West Coast were being relocated to the interior of the U.S and a trickle of Japanese from Hawai'i were being sent to these mainland concentration camps. Yet Joe was an Italian fighting for the U.S. and in subsequent months I met other Italians and Germans who were in the army fighting for America. Why were Japanese-Americans being singled out to be incarcerated behind barbed wire and not Italians and Germans?

A curfew and blackout were strictly enforced, as soldiers with Thompson sub-machine guns patrolled the streets. On occasion, a shot would ring out in the night as a trigger happy G.I. would douse a light with a bullet.

Breaking the rules became a great game for me. I knew the beach and its rocks, gullies and hiding spots like the back of my hand. Sometimes, I would do nighttime favors for my soldier friends. As an example, one night in late April, when all were asleep, I tiptoed out the back door. Sneaking like an Indian being hunted by cowboys, I ran behind fences, over the coastal road, and slid to the beach, my heart thumping as I watched for patrols. Creeping along the sand, I snaked up sandbags protecting a machine gun nest guarding my favorite break in the reef. I wondered why the military placed that 30 caliber Browning machine gun there. The doughboys were defending the shallow water stretching out to sea for several hundred yards. There was no way the Japanese could cross over those sharp coral rocks.

"Pst, Andy. It's me, Bobby, with the stuff."

"Get in here quick, kid," a voice whispered.

I slithered on my tummy down into the nest. There were three soldiers manning the gun and they were all eager to see me. "Have you got it?" asked Andy Gump.

Reaching into my pocket, I pulled out a pack of cigarettes and matches. Eagerly, the men grabbed the cigs and started puffing, the faint reddish glow increasing the natural ruddiness of their faces. Smoking on duty was prohibited, but these were men destined for combat and they were entitled to a few vices.

"Beat it kid, the lieutenant will be making his rounds soon and you better not be here," Andy said, then smiled and handed me a 50 cent piece. Slithering out of the machine gun nest, shuffling low, I ran along the beach heading for home.

None of the soldiers defending Kapa'a beaches realized that there was a Japanese fighting force inland from their positions. Mimicking the machine gun nests that we saw constructed to fight invaders, the neighborhood kids built a bunker at the edge of the Waipouli residences. A large hole was dug into the sand and coconut logs formed a square around it. The top of the bunker was a roof of coconut branches laid over the logs. This was the command post.

Beyond the bunker was a jungle of trees, shrubs, and tall reeds stretching from it to the coconut grove at Wailua, a distance of half a mile. We could not run around with BB guns anymore, so we fashioned sticks to look like rifles and cut inner tubes into bands, then stretched one from the muzzle of the fake gun to a trigger mechanism. The object of the combat was for one group of kids to defend the bunker, and another group to attack it by getting close enough to hurl a small green coconut onto the leaf roof of the fort. Hypothetically, a hit would blow up the bunker.

You could not defend the fortress by hiding inside, but had to find defensive positions in the jungle and shoot the attackers before they could hurl their coconut grenades. Of course, one group of kids had to be the Americans and another group the Japanese. Who better to be the Americans than the Hawaiian boys and who could best imitate Japanese soldiers: the Japanese boys.

Let me tell you that those Japanese guys were the best infiltrators in the business. I got spanked by a rubber band in the butt more than once. Sad to say for the United States, American-Hawaiians kept losing the bunker to the grenades of the American-Japanese. No wonder the 442nd regimental combat team composed of Nisei from Hawai'i, is the most decorated unit in American military history, 18,000 awards for heroism.

All these fighting men needed their shoes shined and when the scrounging became less profitable, polish, brush, cloth and box were acquired. The streets of Kapa'a thronged with men in khaki looking for a beer, for food, for women. There were slim pickings for the latter, but it always paid to have your shoes shined, especially since the duty officer might like that.

The G.I.s gathered in the area around the Roxy where there was food, beer, and the movies. Soon the U.S.O. arrived and opened its doors at the old roller-skate rink diagonally across the street from the theater. Stars came to entertain the soldiers, like Joe E. Brown and Edgar G. Robinson. They brought more military to Kapa'a and to the Roxy. When you had those ingredients, you were bound to have customers for a Hawaiian shoe shine boy.

I walked the area in my khaki shorts, t-shirt, and bare feet, a white box banging at my side. Staring at shoes, I'd point and say, "Shine? Only a dime." The G.I.'s seemed to like a little brown kid and often would put a shoe on my box. I'd start to work, brushing, applying polish with my fingers, spitting on a shoe, then dramatically stretch a cloth with a loud whack, and start the shine. While working, the questions were always the same: "Know any girls? Can you get us some whiskey?" As I think back, maybe the guys didn't want a shine, for the right answer got you a good tip, and the wrong answer...oh well, what did a kid know about those things.

There was good money to be made by shining shoes and often I would return home with my pockets jingling with change. Mother would confiscate the money saying she would put it into a savings account. Sometimes I'd filch a dime and run to the Chinese store to buy firecrackers, and then proceed to blow up the Japanese tin soldiers attacking my sand fort.

With the arrival of thousands of men onto Kaua'i, there was a lack of available women on the island. Even the hugely overweight *wahine* was a raving beauty in a town where the males outnumbered the females by 500 to 1. This produced some humorous sights.

"Hey Mac, want a shine?" I solicited the five soldiers at the bar across the street from the Roxy. "Only a dime," but the five were either too drunk or too enamored with the two large beauties they were trying to seduce. After the men had plied the women with a few drinks, but seemed to fail at romance, the party of seven left the bar and attempted to board the local bus driven by Mice Yoshida who owned the gas station on the Roxy corner.

"Golly," I muttered, "How are those two Ni'ihau women going to get into the bus?"

Mice scratched his head as the first lady attempted to heave her bulk through the door of his conveyance. After several minutes of squeezing and struggling, a solution to the problem was found. Two men got onto the bus and grabbed a pudgy arm as the lady stood sideways. Three soldiers stood outside and pushed against the pounds of flesh. With a pop, the lady squiggled into the vehicle and with a second pop, the other lady entered. Yoshida started up his small bus and it limped towards Lihu'e, tilting at a 45 degree angle.

There were sad moments also, like the time I found the young serviceman drowning in his puke in auntie's front yard. With his arm around me, I brought him to Katie's veranda. Together we washed his face, cleaned him, and put him to bed. Poor kid was just a few years older than I and frightened to death. He was in a strange world; being sent off to die on some "God-forsaken island." To drown his misery, he had drunk too much alcohol. After sleeping it off, we sent him back to war with clean clothes and a teacup of kindness.

Boredom for the troops was inevitable and the need to entertain the men during leave time became a military necessity. From on high, it was decreed that the movies were given military priority, so the flow of film from the mainland to Kaua'i resumed. New movies were coming out of Hollywood, not with the great male stars of the pre-war years, since many of them were in the service, but with some new names. These were actors who would become major stars: John Wayne, a lanky former football player, an over draft age Humphrey Bogart, and the usual assortment of cowboy heroes like Hopalong Cassidy and Tom Mix.

Overnight, W.A. Fernandez's folly became a success. The 1,050 seat theater would fill to capacity on Fridays, Saturdays, and Sundays. W.A. gave discount prices to the servicemen. The military responded by depositing soldiers, sailors, and marines by the truckload at the box office. For months, the Roxy provided the only continuous entertainment in town and was constantly full.

At Christmas 1942, my father closed the door to my bedroom adjacent to the kitchen. I knew something important was happening and I crept to the door. With my ear against it, I could hear my dad say, "Agnes, I paid off the mortgage and we have $50,000 dollars in the bank." I realized then that my father had finally found the pot of gold at the end of the rainbow in Kapa'a.

Sometime after the American naval victory at Midway on June 4, 1942, martial law and blackout rules relaxed. Roxy square began to jump. Movies could be shown at night and Stumpy's hamburger stand, the U.S.O. and other businesses could stay open. Kapa'a no longer rolled up and went to bed at sundown; it would be hopping after midnight. Despite all this activity, Kapa'a was a clean town. Vice was not evident, although I suspect there was a madam working in Kapa'a Heights. Gambling and crime were at a minimum. townspeople were honest, thrifty, and hard working. Above all, a spirit of aloha prevailed.

Residents opened their homes to the young military personnel. If men were sick, they were cared for by the locals. If men had needs that could be honestly and reasonably fulfilled, they were tended to without charge. The Roxy families participated in this aloha spirit. Our homes were places where servicemen could relax, be fed, and entertained.

Many who were homesick and needed friends were given special treatment at the movies. After the war, this aloha would be well remembered by veterans stationed on Kaua'i.

Since the military had priority, rationing was strict. Yet other than gasoline, we were self sufficient. My family had a farm in Wailua house lots where we raised tomatoes, beans, papayas, and other vegetables. At home, we had a chicken and duck yard supplying fresh eggs and poultry to eat or barter. Although the beaches were shut down with barbed wire lining them, we could still fish where it was too rocky for the wire to be anchored. If there was something needed, you traded for it and the soldiers were always generous. Their PX was well stocked with goods.

Kapa'a was a town that had everything: gas stations, plumbing, machine, and repair shops, merchandise stores, mom and pop groceries, and two movie theaters, Pono and the Roxy. There were cattle and dairy farms in the hinterland, with taro and rice fields nearby.

With the rolling back of the Japanese threat in the Pacific, sugar cane and pineapple could be harvested and product shipped out. With "Pono" cannery in Kapa'a and what was called "Up" cannery in Kapahi, there was work to do and money to be made.

Behind Sleeping Giant Mountain, the military built a huge training complex. Upwards of 15,000 U.S. soldiers lived beneath Wai'ale'ale mountain, in an area that would later become the location for the filming of *Jurassic Park*. I learned that these men were preparing for the invasion of the Philippines. They were youths from the mainland that had never seen a jungle or an ocean. Drowning and injuries were inevitable.

Our family befriended many of these men. During the invasion of the Philippines, we received poignant letters from our soldier friends telling of their hardships and loneliness. Saddest of all were the death reports. Oh, I wish that Pearl Harbor had never happened and that Kaua'i could have remained a blissful paradise. For war is cruel and you lose to it people you care about. Yet change is inevitable, often occurring because of war.

In Europe, Hitler's Germany was being smashed by Russian armies attacking in the east and American and British forces hammering German divisions defending the Rhine. In the skies over Berlin, bombs rained down on Hitler's bunker to eradicate the evil genius who had begun the most devastating of the planet's wars. A new German fighter, the Messerschmitt 262 jet aircraft, was seeking to wrest away air superiority from the hardy, piston-driven Mustang P51, an airplane that had given America air dominance since mid-1944. Few realized, as swirling dog fights erupted over Germany, that the jet age had begun.

In the Pacific, the Japanese Imperial Navy was pulverized, its air force destroyed. Super fortresses rained incendiaries on Tokyo flaming the bamboo city into ruin. The end of war was near when Germany surrendered on May 8, 1945. For Japan, its last defense from invasion was the kamikaze, suicide bombers who attacked American ships knowing they would die. The U.S. military took this threat seriously. Our troops had lost thousands of men in Okinawa and Iwo Jima to fanatical enemy soldiers. A final attack on the main Japanese Islands would be a blood bath, with millions of civilians becoming kamikaze to save their homeland.

President Harry Truman made the momentous decision to drop the only two atomic bombs America had on Hiroshima and Nagasaki. He did it to save American and Japanese lives and to end the war. Whatever historians might say about this decision, it produced the desired result, the unconditional surrender of Japan.

On September 2, 1945, a Japanese delegation signed the peace documents on the deck of the battleship *Missouri*. With war's end, the flood of American fighting men receded from Kaua'i's shores. Kapa'a and the Roxy returned to its pre-war condition. Traffic through town normalized and moved again at island speeds. Khaki-clad servicemen disappeared from town, as did shoe shine boys, the U.S.O. and some bars. Yet, the legacy of the war was still with us in the form of abandoned military vehicles, barracks, barbed wire-girded shores, and gun emplacements rusting in the ocean air.

W.A.'s folly had been a wartime financial success. The Roxy was full during the war years, and the dream of Agnes and W.A. Fernandez provided them financial security. Others in Kapa'a profited by the war as well, men like George Kondo who became the soda water king of Kaua'i. In the hinterland, farms and ranches had grown huge supplying the food needs of soldiers and civilians.

With prosperity, my parents left for San Francisco to enjoy the cool, crisp breezes of the bayside city. They went there to return to school. Work as a *paniolo* and a pineapple cutter had ended their education. In retirement, Agnes and W.A. finally had the leisure time to learn reading, writing, and arithmetic.

In the years following the war, there was a slow drift away from Kapa'a by the Chinese and Japanese to start new lives in Honolulu. I remained in Hawai'i to attend Kamehameha Schools. Although movies were still the main entertainment medium in Kapa'a, the days of the overflow wartime crowds were gone forever. It seemed in that post war year, that Kaua'i had returned to the lazy, peaceful days of the tin canoe and the *hukilau*.

Chapter 14

Tsunami

A tidal wave is misnamed, for it is not a wave created by the action of tides, instead; it is a wave created by a great seismic disturbance under the sea. Such a quake causes a sudden vertical displacement of part of the ocean floor. This rift acts like a bellows, sucking in and blowing out sea water with tremendous force. In the open sea, this seismic-produced wave can crest up to 300 miles long and achieve speeds of 600 miles per hour. It has such a gentle slope, three to four feet, that ships at sea and passing airplanes cannot detect it.

This low wave, on reaching shallow coastal waters, grows to terrifying height caused by abrupt slowing as it reaches land. This braking action magnifies the size of the wave, unleashing it onto the shore with awesome destructive force.

In the frigid waters of the Aleutians, just past midnight on April 1, 1946, a seismic disturbance occurred on the ocean floor. A gigantic wave, 100 feet high, crashed into Scotch Cape on the island of Unimak, and then sped towards Hawai'i. Four hours later, it hit the islands with devastating force. Boats, fishing villages, bridges, buildings, trees, animals, and scores of people were swept to sea, never to be seen again.

Later in the year, I visited the north shore of Kaua'i. At Kalihiwai Bay there were stumps of homes where friends had been engulfed by the raging water and dragged out to sea. In Hanalei there was devastation, the beach and valley was choked with boulders, smashed trees, and broken buildings spread in jumbles all over the sand and taro fields. It appeared that the north shore had been destroyed by an atomic bomb, and would never recover from this catastrophe. Nature had created a line of destruction bisecting the island into two parts, the area north of Kapa'a pulverized and returning to primitive days, the land to the south continuing to be prosperous.

There were other tsunamis that struck in 1946. These waves would sweep away the plantations, canneries, and political structure of the islands, leaving in their wake the new economy and politics of Hawai'i.

In *Gone with the Wind*, Margaret Mitchell wrote of a plantation-rich minority who lived in gracious wealth, whose lives were forever changed by the devastation of the Civil War. That war was not fought for ideals, like freeing the slaves, but because of economics: the survival of cotton producing plantations. The politicians on both sides, who caused the war to occur, could not foresee the economic and social changes that would be wrought by victory for the North and defeat for the South.

Wendell Willkie, the defeated Republican candidate for president in 1940, was sent by Roosevelt on a round-the-world fact-finding trip. When he returned to America, Willkie wrote a book entitled, *One World*. This concept, that we are not isolated dots on a map but interrelated and integral parts of the whole, is the economic and social legacy of World War II. Because of that war, we found that forevermore, none of us in our islands are, "...entire unto ourselves, we are all one, a part of the main." (John Donne, *For Whom the Bell Tolls)*

Hitler had begun his war in Europe to acquire *Lebensraum*, living space. He believed that Germany would become a Great Power with land and Slavic slaves in a subjugated Russia. In the Pacific, the military junta ruling Japan believed that their country could only achieve its ambitions by conquering oil and mineral-rich Southeast Asia. None of these men envisioned the consequences of defeat nor did the victors appreciate the aftermath of global war.

As the ocean tsunami receded, a building wave of labor unrest, restrained during the war by martial law, flooded over Hawai'i. Harry Bridges, president of the ILWU, ordered a strike designed to improve the wages and living conditions of thousands of workers. This mainland union had come to Hawai'i and catalyzed its laborers into a powerful force that radically changed the business climate.

Bridges was Australian-born and for several of the war years the federal government had sought his deportation as a Communist for his outspoken support of organized labor. At the time of the strike he had just won a major victory before the United States Supreme Court which had overturned his deportation order and upheld his right to speak freely, a right, the Court said, "...guaranteed by the United States Constitution."

It was a long and acrimonious strike, but labor won. Wages and benefits improved to the point that sugar workers in Hawai'i eventually became the highest paid in the world. After the strike was settled, Bridges declared, "Hawai'i is no longer a feudal colony." In succeeding years, Bridges, Jack Hall, and other union leaders in the islands would be prosecuted as Communists.

In 1946, another wave was building. Japanese-Americans, introduced to politics by the war, took advantage of the G.I. Bill and educated themselves in law as well as other professions. Returning Nisei were determined to effectuate change in Hawai'i.

Since annexation in 1898, conservative Republicans and the "Big Five," had controlled the Territory in every aspect of its life. With war's end, Hawai'i was no longer isolated nor a feudal enclave separated from the rest of the world. An eight-year struggle for dominance of the political structure of the islands ensued, culminating in the election of the first Democratic controlled legislature in 1954.

For several years, the economy of post-war Kaua'i remained dependent on sugar cane and pineapple. Unlike Europe and Japan, the infrastructure of the islands had not been damaged. Sugar plantations and pineapple canneries were intact and could easily meet world demand. Yet, like the end of slavery in the South after the Civil War, the exploitation of labor in Hawai'i ended with the strike of 1946. Though the workers gained economically, the agricultural businesses suffered. Sugar plantations and pineapple canneries died. Their demise was not sudden, like a tsunami, but slow.

As wages improved and jobs shrank, the crowds at the Roxy dwindled. The hot spot during the war years, Kapa'a, returned to its quiet pre-war state. Like the plantations, the Roxy bled as profits evaporated.

W.A. Fernandez passed away in San Francisco in September of 1949. He had the biggest funeral in the history of Kapa'a as mourners from all over Kaua'i came to pay their respects to the itinerant Hawaiian who had become a premier showman of the Pacific. He died at a time when his beloved Roxy was still a movie theater that he could be proud of.

Chapter 15

Television

For fifty years, the creations of Marey, Edison, and the Lumiere brothers provided Americans with their prime source of entertainment, the movies. Hardly noticed in 1923 was the invention of the iconoscope by Vladimir Zworykin. Yet it was this device, a scanning tube for a television camera, and the subsequent creation of a cathode-ray tube capable of reproducing a broadcast picture, that were to revolutionize the entertainment industry of the world. By the purchase of a box with a tube and supporting electrical apparatus, every home could become a theater.

Britain was in the forefront of the television industry in the decade before World War II. New Yorkers were electrified by the first BBC televised broadcast from London in November of 1936. At the 1939 World's Fair, a fledgling television company, N.B.C., inaugurated the first regular broadcasts of high definition images, television.

With the advent of World War II, British and American T.V. broadcasting stopped due to wartime restrictions. Curiously, the Nazis opened a station in Paris in 1942 to televise their version of the war.

With peace, broadcasting resumed in Europe and America; this new entertainment medium swept across the continent. On December 1, 1952, moving and speaking images, sent by oscillating waves through the air, came to Hawai'i. No longer was it necessary to leave the home to be entertained for a price, at a movie theater. By the purchase of an electric box with a magic lantern apparatus inside, a family could remain home and be entertained by Uncle Miltie, Arthur Godfrey, Hopalong Cassidy, and various other actors and actresses.

Television caused panic among the omnipotent movie moguls who had controlled Hollywood for decades. Competitive pressure from this new communications media forced producers to come up with creative innovations to induce audiences to return to the movies. Wide-screen processes, stereophonic sound systems, and three-dimensional cinematography were all tried in frantic attempts to wean customers away from their homes and back to the theater.

New technology required the Roxy to acquire this wizardry to survive. Yet old customers did not buy into these glitzy visual wares. They remained at home watching T.V.

Bleeding from the costs of keeping up, Roxy's financial deterioration accelerated. The family poured money into improvements without a commensurate return at the box office. Competition between the N.B.C. peacock and the M.G.M. lion had an unexpected benefit, movie moguls looked to their past to find answers to beat the analog wave competition.

In 1911, the movie industry had relocated from barnyard studios and the scenery-deficient locales of New Jersey and New York to sunny Southern California. In Los Angeles, wages were cheaper, and land inexpensive. At a roadhouse called "Nestor" in Hollywood, the first movie studio was built.

Los Angeles had another attraction. Within walking distance were all the scenic locations needed to crank out movies of romance, drama, comedy and adventure. The superb natural locales of the San Bernardino hills made it an excellent place to produce movies like *Shangri-La.*

Although directors occasionally sought exotic natural locales to make their movies, such as *Dangerous Innocence,* filmed in Hawai'i in 1925, most cinemas were produced in back lot studios and locales near Los Angeles. It was cheaper.

Early television shows were telecast in studio settings. Movie directors realized that filming in exotic true-to-life locales, and in places popularized by World War II, might induce audiences to leave their cathode-ray sets and return to the theaters. Movie moguls rediscovered Kaua'i and its spectacular mountains rising from the sea. It is a great natural locale to film pictures like: *Ms. Sadie Thompson, Pagan Love Song, Bird of Paradise, South Pacific, and Blue Hawai'i.*

Kaua'i had what movie directors call "paint," a beautiful tropical setting of steep mountains, waterfalls, beaches, trees, and flowers in a wide range of colors. You could use up thousands of gallons of paint on a back lot sound stage and never capture the natural beauty of the Garden Island.

The Roxy played a role in the filming. Academy Award-winning cinematographer, Leon Shamroy, needed to view the daily filming of his Bali Hai scenes from *South Pacific.* The only theater on the island that had the state-of-the-art equipment demanded by the movie was the

Roxy. Each day, the rushes photographed by Shamroy were previewed at the theater. This small financial triumph was pyrrhic, for the money earned from the daily previewing of the movie could not make up for the expense of the innovations. Moviegoers continued to dwindle until the 1,050 seat theater was projecting its wares to a handful of patrons. Despite the Roxy's financial troubles, the beautiful scenes of *South Pacific* and the attention focused on Hawai'i by the attack on Pearl Harbor brought to the islands its economic salvation.

Chapter 16

Tourism

A Martin M-130 flying boat, aptly named the "Hawaiian Clipper," made the first commercial flight to Hawai'i in 1936. There were seven passengers on board and the flight took 21 hours and 20 minutes. In pre-war days, tourism to Hawai'i was just a trickle. It was limited by the passenger capacity of the Pan American Clipper and the tourist capacity of the *Matsonia* and *Lurline*. These were ships which could comfortably transport 600 visitors on a five day voyage from California to Hawai'i. This trickle of tourists did little to help Hawai'i's economy, yet the weekly visits of the two white ships of the Matson Navigation Company created exciting, nostalgic memories for anyone who has ever seen a docking and debarkation of passengers at Aloha Tower.

I recall paddling in a canoe to greet the *Lurline*, strewing flowers in its path as it sailed into Honolulu. Diving for pennies in the rippling water while the ship eased into its mooring, I wondered if the Scotsmen standing at the railing of the ship wore underpants beneath their kilts. On the dock above me, the Royal Hawaiian Band played a John Philip Sousa march and then switched to a poignant Hawaiian melody. Sweet-scented flower *lei* and people were everywhere. On the pier, beautiful longhaired hula maids, skimpily clothed in leaf skirts and coconut shell bras, swayed to the rhythms of Hawaiian music provided by musicians plunking guitars and ukuleles. The colorful bedlam, chaos, and aloha on the arrival of these Matson ships are forever memorable.

As I have mentioned, the Messerschmitt 262 was one of the most fearsome fighter aircraft of World War II. Its speed was phenomenal and rate of climb outstanding. Had it been produced in sufficient numbers and put to earlier use as a fighter aircraft, these jets could have turned the tide of the European air war in favor of the Axis. Yet when Hitler first saw a prototype of the ME 262 in 1943, he ordered it redesigned as a bomber. The Nazi dictator did not believe in defense, only destructive offense.

The turbo jet engine, designed by Willy Messerschmitt and perfected in Britain, revolutionized the world's tourist industry. These engines could push aircraft for longer distances and they were cheaper, quieter, and faster than conventional radial powered planes. *Qantas* was the first airline to bring commercial jet aircraft to Hawai'i in 1959. The trip took five hours and the price was affordable. In the first year of operation, 250,000 tourists flew to the islands.

Other airlines sought passenger routes to Hawai'i and once they were established, tourism began a steady rise towards its present day prominence as the economic backbone of the 50th State. As in the days of Jack London, Robert Louis Stevenson and Mark Twain, the lure of the tropics drew people from all over the world to, "the finest fleet of islands that ever sailed in any sea."

At the same time that thousands of tourists came to Hawai'i, its agricultural economy faltered. Labor and shipping costs were high and island grown products could not compete in the world market. Plantations and canneries shut down.

In 1962, Hawaiian Cannery and the American Can Company in Kapa'a closed. Great fields of pineapple and sugar cane that had carpeted the low hills below Sleeping Giant, Wai'ale'ale and Anahola Mountains slowly returned to nature. Beyond Anahola, on the way to Kilauea, tall saccharum grass still grew. Yet its processing plant, Kilauea Sugar Company, tottered. All too soon, even this plantation succumbed to the overseas competition.

Tourism thrived on Waikiki and Mau'i, but languished on Kaua'i. These grim economic facts, closures of plantations and a lack of tourists appeared to spell doom for the town of Kapa'a. The few visitors that came to the island drove through, heading for the mysterious "Bali Hai" country in Hanalei.

As more and more movies were made on Kaua'i, curious visitors came to the Garden Island to find the lagoon where Elvis Presley warbled *Blue Hawai'i*, or visit the beach where Mitzi Gaynor sang, "*I'm Going to Wash That Man Right Out of My Hair*." There had only been the Lihu'e Inn in 1952, but in succeeding years, Coco Palms at Wailua, Hanalei Plantation, the Kaua'i Surf at Kalapaki Beach, and other hotels soon opened.

Increasing tourism brought economic health back to Kapa'a. This new prosperity was not directly tourist based, for many visitors continued to pass through the town going north in search of movie sites. What attracted people to Kapa'a was land that could be acquired by hotel employees, blue collar workers, and newcomers at reasonable prices. Most important, the community welcomed them.

With the passing of pineapple and sugar cane, the financial deterioration of the Roxy accelerated. Like an aged warrior, it continued to rear proudly above Kapa'a town, but its exterior became shabby with age and the effects of the weather. Chinese *Kung Fu* movies gave it a shot in the arm for a short period, but this was still not enough to save it from closing its doors to the magic of the movies.

Chapter 17

The Gods Laugh

Thetis bathed her son in the River Styx to make him immortal. Because the river into Hades was so swift, and for fear of losing her son to it, she held him by his heel. Achilles' immortality derived from this bathing, allowed him to win many battles until Paris discovered his fatal weakness. When Paris' arrow slew Achilles by piercing his heel, the gods on Olympus laughed at humans who try to achieve immortality.

In the 1960's, the poor of Kingston, Jamaica, became intrigued by the writhing rhythm of American "soul" music. Springy, offbeat tunes began to rock the streets and discos of Jamaica. Bob Marley, the Wailers, and the Toots popularized Reggae and its offshoot, Rastafarian music. In the late 1980's, Reggae came to the Roxy. The downstairs auditorium was partially cleared of seats; the stage and sound system beefed up. The rocking rhythm of Jamaica arrived in Kapa'a. Once again, the theater filled with happy lovers; it was standing room only as the "soul" music of Kingston blared its beat throughout the town. Never before in its history had the Roxy experienced such rocking and stomping.

Unfortunately, Reggae groups seldom came to Kaua'i and interest in this new sound had a limited audience. Without regular performances, the Roxy deteriorated. Physical damage from Hurricane Iwa in 1982 was not fully repaired. The tropical climate corroded the theater's tin roof which needed constant attention to prevent rain damage. Besieged by all of these factors, its strength sapped, the Roxy's mortality became more and more evident.

W.A. Fernandez had struggled all of his life. He had traveled the roadways and sea lanes from Hanalei to Yokohama, showing his movies. Over the years, he planned for his future theater, going to the United States, gaining ideas from the world beyond the "dot" in the Pacific. Overcoming all obstacles, W.A, of Hawaiian-Portuguese extraction, and his wife Agnes, of Hawaiian-Alsatian blood, acquired land and constructed the Roxy in 1939. It was a remarkable achievement for two Euro-Hawaiians.

Yet, W.A. left an unprotected heel when he built his theater. For ten thousand dollars more, he could have constructed the Roxy of concrete and, like the pyramids, it might have withstood the test of time. Strapped for cash, W.A. chose to build the structure with an auditorium of wood and a roof of tin.

By early September of 1992, the Roxy still rose three stories above town, the tallest building in Kapa'a. You saw it as you entered, its great height surpassing the loftiest of palm trees. This landmark had won many battles over the elements. It escaped intact the great flood of 1940, the tidal wave of April Fool's Day, 1946, Hurricane Dot in 1959, and Iwa in 1982.

Within sight of the Roxy, Steven Spielberg filmed scenes for his dinosaur epic, *Jurassic Park*. It was a sad moment for the Roxy because its reggae-gutted innards and out-of-date technology made it incapable of providing a proper setting for viewing the early rushes of Spielberg's movie.

The film brought to life the Saurischian Dinosaurs composed of two groups: 1) the herbivorous Sauropodomorpha, creatures with long necks allowing them to consume vegetation from the tallest trees; and 2) the carnivorous Theropoda. These tyrant-lizards were the most fearsome creatures spawned on earth. With its 45 foot length, 20 foot height, and massive jagged-tooth jaws, T-Rex was the featured monster of *Jurassic Park*.

In Spielberg's adventure movie, billed as "*65 Million Years in the Making*," Tyrannosaurus Rex tore down fences, flattened trees, smashed buildings and overturned vehicles as it rampaged across movie screens all over the world. For many months in 1992, Spielberg and crew filmed on Kaua'i. By September 8, the movie, *Jurassic Park*, was nearly completed. Scenes of an outdoor restaurant in Costa Rica were being shot at Kapa'a beach outside an old metal warehouse painted in the bright colors of the rainbow. The weather that day was overcast and muggy.

Hurricanes are aptly named after Huracan, a Carib god of evil. They are violent cyclones originating in tropical oceans. The most important factors for their creation are hot, humid air at low levels and the huge reservoir of heat energy that a warm tropical ocean provides. Warm seas in the summer and fall plus an intense tropical depression over a portion of ocean can cause winds to be sucked into the low pressure area, become further warmed and whirl upwards in cyclonic fashion at speeds of 75 to 150 miles per hour. At the hurricane's center is an area of cloudless skies and gentle winds; this can be 12 to 40 miles across and take many minutes to pass through any location stricken by the ocean-created whirlwind. From satellite pictures, a hurricane appears as a whirlpool of clouds being sucked into a black eye. Tropical hurricanes are notorious for their sudden changes in speed, intensity, and direction.

In August of 1992, Hurricane Andrew struck Florida, Louisiana, and Mississippi. It left thousands homeless and caused billions of dollars in damage. In early September 1992, the wind, *makani,* was building up its strength in the warm seas south of Hawai'i. As its power transformed itself from the gentle *makani 'olu 'olu* to the powerful *makani ikaka*, hurricane warnings were issued to the Hawaiian Islands. O'ahu girded for its fury as the eye of the storm moved inexorably in its direction. Kaua'i appeared to be safe from the mounting fury of the wind, but *La'amaomao* was either fickle or angry at the Garden Island. Capriciously and without adequate warning, the goddess of the wind hurled *'ena makani* at Kaua'i.

The hurricane struck the island like a hundred mile-wide phalanx of a billion tyrant-lizards. Fences were torn down, telephone poles flattened, trees uprooted, buildings smashed, and vehicles overturned. Stephen Spielberg's great imagination could not have dreamed of such rapid massive destruction, nor recreate it on the movie screen. The eye of the storm began to pass over Kaua'i. Its calm caused people hiding beneath mattresses and inside buildings to leave their homes, believing the tempest was over. *La'amaomao* was not finished. The eye passed over Kapa'a heading north; as it did, *makani* rose again in intensive fury destroying all in its path. Screaming winds in the whirlpool of clouds swirling about Iniki's eye gusted at speeds up to 160 miles per hour.

A *venturi* tube draws fuel into a carburetor by the vacuum caused by liquids being pressured through a constricted space. Powerful winds, swirling around an enclosed building, may be drawn in through tiny cracks in its roof. Once inside, the wild contained winds seek to exit through the entry cracks. The built-up pressure of the winds in the confined space can hurl the building's roof from its fastenings. Then, as the winds roar out through the roofless structure, the *venturi* effect occurs. A momentary vacuum is created within the building and there is no air pressure to support the walls. With the roof gone and the vacuum created inside, outside winds will crush the building.

Iniki charged at the Roxy, its winds gusting at incredible speeds. *Makani* found the Achilles heel of the theater; it worried away a tiny section of the old, sun-damaged metal and whirled inside, then swirled out just as quickly. Like an exploding Vesuvius, the escaping winds blew off the roof; a thousand potential tin canoes soared over Kapa'a town. Roofless and without air support for the walls of the auditorium of the Roxy, *ena makani* crushed the *ma kai* wall inwards. Ironically, spared from serious damage was the concrete forward part of the building.

Soon the winds moderated, and *ua lani pili* descended from the heavens. For weeks, it poured rain into the roofless theater, completing the destruction of the Roxy. Iniki devastated Kaua'i, causing more than two billion dollars in physical damage. It was the single greatest property disaster in Hawai'i's history; fortunately, unlike the killer tsunami of 1946, human life was spared. But the misery inflicted by *La'amaomao* was widespread and long lasting.

Sadly, expert examination of the structure provided no hope for the theater's survival. On a bright day in November 1992, great machines pushed down the Roxy. The remnants of W.A.'s dream were hauled to a nameless grave, the outlines of the building and its concrete flooring were covered over by rock, earth, and grass. The Roxy has now disappeared except in the folklore of Hawaiian history. Its former existence gives mute testimony to a two hundred year struggle of Hawaiians attempting to cope with a changing world, this struggle only succeeding with the infusion of blood and ideas of people from foreign lands. Its attestation of this truth is left in the words and pictures of the two people who built the Roxy Theater.

The legendary Giant sleeping after too much awa juice.

A luau for the neighborhood at Grandpa Scharsch's home in Kapa'a. Mother Agnes standing in background, smiling at children of all races.

Kapa'a School, 8th Grade Graduating Class, 1921. Front row, far right, Helen Morgan Rodrigues. After 8th grade, you went to work in the cannery or plantation. Higher education choices were Kaua'i High School or Honolulu.

Graduation, 1951, Mrs. Sheldon's preschool. Cousin Linda Paik, top row far left.

Cousin Linda Paik Moriarity, center. "Hula Keiki," performing at a May Day event on a Kapa'a Beach.

First grade class, Kapa'a School, Cousin Helen Morgan Rodrigues, teacher.

Hanamaulu School. Grade Eight at Lihue Airport. Lihue, Kauai. T.H. Mar 3 1934

Hawaiian Airlines began operation in 1929, with an 8 passenger Sikorsky S-38 Amphibian. Initially, passengers were transported by canoe to and from the airplane. Upon water landing, some passengers received a salt water drenching before getting their floral lei.

Before taking the amphibian aircraft, W.A. Fernandez prepares to board. The men are ready to be doused by sea water and protected from the cold air while flying.

Agnes Scharsch Fernandez, after dad's death, heading around the world.
Early 1960s.

From Left to Right: Alice Morgan Paik, Linda Paik (Moriarty), Catherine Scharsch Morgan and Agnes Scharsch Fernandez. Linda's graduation from 8th grade, Kapa'a School.

Typical Kapa'a plantation style home.

Auntie Eileen Smith's plantation house, Kapa'a, Kaua'i, 1969. Eventually
destroyed by Hurricane Iniki on September 11th, 1992.

Aerial view Kapa'a shoreline taken July 4th, 1924. Foreground: Hawaiian Canneries and Waia'kea Stream, site of Dracula's coffin. Center: Shoreline of Waipouli and cleared area for future subdivision where the Hawaiian shoeshine boy was born. Center, along the main highway: site of All Saints Church where the Fighting 69th was first bivouacked. These Irish soldiers defended the beach from Japanese invaders. Center Right: labor camp for the Makee Sugar Plantation workers.

The heart of Kapa'a from 1913 to 1962, was Hawaiian Canneries Company, Ltd. and American Can Company. Today, it is the site of the Pono Kai Resort. Behind the white Hawaiian Church in the background is the 3-story Roxy Theater. Kapa'a Town's population during the 1940s was approximately 2,300. Of that number, 900 were cannery employees.

Kapa'a Flood, 1940. Top, looking toward the center of town. Bottom, main highway by the Hongwanji Mission just south of Waia'kea Stream.

Taken from the Kapa'a scenic lookout. The shore is being swept by heavy pounding surf around the time of Hurricane Dot.

The Kealia Theater after Hurricane Dot struck in 1959.

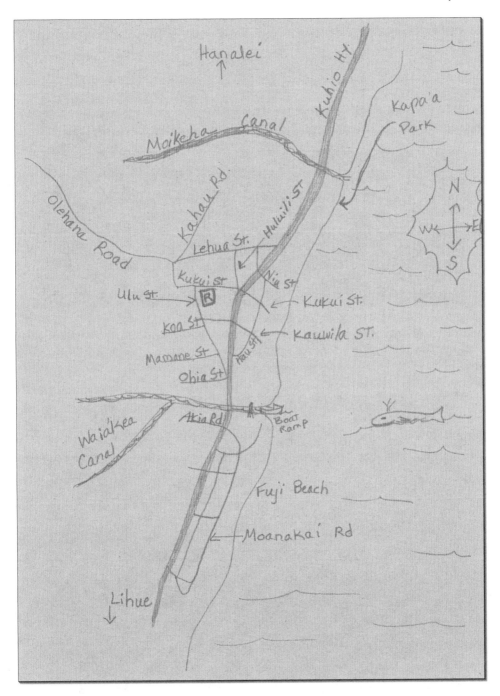

Kapa'a Town Map, Courtesy of Judith Fernandez

Intersection of Kukui and Kuhio Highway 1969. On the left in the background is the Roxy. On the corner to the left is Yoshida gas station, present site of the ABC store.

The intersection of Kuhio Hwy. and Kukui St. Behind the ABC store, the Roxy Theater once stood. 2009 Photo.

The author at three years old in front of family home, 1032 Kealoha Street, Waipouli, Kaua'i

Off to first grade at Kapa'a School. Barefoot and ready to learn, I say aloha to Auntie Katie and cat Nellie

In Aunt Katie's front yard. Six years old and thinking of how to get out of my chores.

My grandfather's path to work at Makee Plantation in Kealia, in the good old days of transportation. When a train crossed this bridge, kids grabbed cane stalks from the passing cars and were often dragged along by the slow moving engine. When not filching cane, we played chicken with the oncoming train. A quick dive into the stream was often necessary to escape the huffing and puffing steam locomotive.

My sister, Colleen Fernandez Jensen, High School graduation, 1944.

Kamehameha Schools, senior class photo, 1949.

Appointed by Governor Ronald Reagan to the Superior Court, California.

Clockwise from the top: Bill, Donald, Jon, and Robert Fernandez. The Kolohe Kids, aka Rascals in Paradise

Extended Scharsch family at Lydgate Beach Park 1969.

My last visit with Don Ho, shortly before his death. Top left, his wife Haumea, Bill and Don.

My Kamehameha School classmate, "Quack," our nickname for Don Ho. At R.O.T.C summer camp in Sacramento, we debuted as a duet and failed miserably. After his military service, Don went on to become an iconic Hawaiian entertainer and I became a judge.

"Talking Story" on the family porch at 1032 Kealoha St., Waipouli, Kaua'i.

My ku'uipo, Judie, and I before my grandmother's Hawaiian flag quilt. Historically, Hawaiians made these quilts to protest the loss of their sovereignty by annexation to the United States. The quilts were hidden from the eyes of Westerners. Depicted is the combination of the American flag red, white, and blue stripes, the British Union Jack, and the Royal Kahili in the middle.

The Morgan home property: Foreground: Takemoto Photography Shop, a rental property, and back building, the sewing room where the Scharsch women met.

"The Sewing Room," where the Aunties, while quilting, decided the families' future: bringing Aunt Eileen from Atlanta, Georgia, during the height of WWII, planning weddings, luaus, and future education for the keiki of the family. All decisions took place in this room and all spoken in Hawaiian to confuse the known eavesdroppers underneath the house.

The sewing room today with two Scharsch descendants, Bill and Linda, reliving fond memories. When the Aunties came out of the sewing room issuing verdicts to the keiki, it was like being at the Vatican while the Cardinals were in conclave deciding the succession of the next Pope. The Aunties would emerge like flying smoke, issuing decrees. Nobody dared argue with them. Their words were kapu.

Epilogue

Waves, winds, fires, and economic disasters have swept Kapa'a during my family's one hundred and ten year relationship with the town. Yet, it has survived these calamities and remains the decent, clean, beautiful place that I grew up in, four score years ago.

Why is Kapa'a such a wonderful place to live and work? Foremost, it did not start as a plantation town controlled by the sugar owner. Instead, Kapa'a was a community where a poor immigrant could acquire land and prosper in freedom. These key facts attracted to it the polyglot of races who retired from work in the sugar fields.

In other areas of the world, multi-cultures do not mix. War and racial violence are not uncommon. Why didn't that happen in Kapa'a? Haven Kuboyama provides the answer, "In the old days, no matter the nationality, we were all struggling to survive. Everybody helped each other. It was the good days."

This aloha spirit continues to this day. Realtor Don Pixler said, "Kapa'a is the best place to live. It has amazing people, the best people of any place. People here will help you. They care about you."

A gracious Thai woman said, "Kapa'a is better than Thailand. There is no chance in my old country to live a beautiful life. In this town you have opportunity, and if you have integrity and skill, you are rewarded for your ability."

"Kapa'a has a healing spirituality," said Robin, a forty year old realtor from California. "I was addicted to alcohol when I came here many years ago to visit a friend. My life was in shambles and I was desperate. After I arrived, I woke at four o'clock in a fog. My mind clouded by my addiction, I stumbled outside and tried to see the beauty around me, but my eyes would not focus. Yet I felt something. Maybe it was the wind or the sound of crashing waves, but I felt something. Sobbing, I fell to my knees and tried to clear my eyes. As my vision returned, I realized that I had been destroying myself. I vowed to give up alcohol. I have been dry ever since. This is a healing, spiritual place that I have tried to leave twice, and I am always pulled back."

Next to Robin stood Linda from Pittsburg, Pennsylvania, who added, "I agree. I was attracted to Kapa'a because my friend told me that it is spiritual. I have been in this town nineteen years and it is the most spiritual place in the world."

These testimonials do not complete the picture of Kapa'a. Walking along the bike path that follows the coastline from Waipouli to Donkey Beach in Kealia, I see the island shining in beauty. Happy children giggle in the tidal pond by my home, warm breezes envelop me, and the restless ocean, wrinkled by foaming waves, is mesmerizing. Tensions flee, stress disappears, and I am *sans souci, without cares.*

There have been changes in the town. The Chinese have left with their pots of gold for Honolulu. The Filipino pool halls, barber shops, and taxi dance auditorium are gone. There are still Japanese merchants and a smattering of Hawaiian shops, but most significant are the number of small businesses run by Caucasians. These are the young people who came to Kaua'i to surf, work in construction, or, as tourists, fell in love with the island. They chose the area of Kapa'a to live for its available, affordable housing, and the "amazing quickness that you get to know everybody."

Kapa'a will continue to prosper in the years ahead for all of the reasons I have mentioned. It had a unique beginning, as a town free of the feudalism of the plantation, where impoverished races could succeed.

Today Kapa'a has lost its pineapple cannery. In its place is the Pono Kai Resort. The once popular beach is eroding, as waves and wind tear away the shoreline, destroying the ironwood forest that once protected it. The marshlands have been drained, filled, and transformed into parks and affordable housing. Wailana swamp has disappeared and the two canals that flow into the sea ensure that Kapa'a will not be flooded.

Though the Roxy is landfill, I have fond memories of it. Among the most poignant, the Filipino man, calling himself Tom Mix, who would come into town dressed like a cowboy. Standing by the ticket booth, with his toy six shooters and ten gallon hat, he would stare at the poster actresses. Selecting one, Tom Mix would kiss the cardboard beauty and say, "I want dis one. Give you money. You get for me."

Or the balmy nights after a movie, when I'd walk across the street to the roller rink, buckle on skates, and skim the concrete to the tune of, "*Roll out the barrel. We'll have a barrel of fun.*" Finished, I'd hop to Stumpy's for a hamburger and coke, then to bed.

Or the days when outside the theater, I'd shine shoes and the G.I.'s would teach me about life: gambling, drinking, and other things.

Or those special moments when the movies transported you to places far away, like a Kansas farm and Munchkin land. As I have told you, after that special movie, I climbed the tallest tree and sang, "*Over the Rainbow.*"

Kapa'a has rainbows bending over it. In the town, my parents found their pot of gold. Many others who left the plantations and came to Kapa'a have made their fortunes and departed. There are newbies who have come from mainland America seeking the spirituality of Kapa'a. Others will come, for a stress-free life is more important than gold.

Though *makani* has destroyed the theater, the Fernandez family has made a new beginning in Kapa'a with a small shopping center, Roxy Square, dedicated to the memory of W.A. and Agnes Fernandez and their implausible achievement for two Hawaiians.

Ewe hanau o ka aina. E'olu I ka mea I'loa'a ho'oko'ana.
Hao ko ala ka makani la, pau loa.
Make no ke kalo a ola I ka palili.

Natives of the land. Be content with what you have achieved.
For with one great sweep of wind, all is gone.
Yet although the taro dies, it lives again in the young plants that it produces.

Index

ROXY THEATRE
BALCONY
ADMIT ONE
GOOD THIS DATE ONLY
The management reserves the right
to revoke the license granted with this
ticket by refunding purchase price.
This ticket is sold with the under-
standing that it is for the FIRST
SHOW ONLY.

ROXY THEATRE
BALC.
CENTER